Words of

Ahikar

Scriptural Research Institute

Published by Digital Ink Productions, 2024

Copyright

Words of Ahikar

Second edition. March 7, 2024

Copyright © 2024 Scriptural Research Institute.

ISBN: 978-1-998288-60-1

The Septuagint was translated into Greek at the Library of Alexandria between 250 and 132 BCE.

The Words of Ahikar was written sometime before 500 BCE. This English translation was created by the Scriptural Research Institute in 2020 and 2022.

The image used for the cover is an artistic reinterpretation of "The Defeat of Sennacherib" by Peter Paul Rubens, painted in 1614. The original painting is currently on display in the Alte Pinakothek, in Munich.

TABLE OF CONTENTS

TABLE OF CONTENTS

II

FORWARD

The Words of Ahikar is the oldest surviving Israelite story, with known copies in Aramaic dating back to the 5th century BCE. As it has been translated into many languages over the past two and a half millennia, it now has several names and translations, including the Words of Ahiqar, the Story of Ahikar, and various variations of the name, including Achiacharos, from the Greek translation, Åḥyqr from the Aramaic translation, Akyrios from the Old Slavonic translation, Ḥayqār from the Arabic translation, and Xikar from the Armenian translation. This translation uses the most common English variation of Ahikar, which is based on a transliteration of the oldest surviving Aramaic version of the name. The oldest fragments of this book found to date, were discovered in Elephantine, Egypt, and date to the 5th century BCE, making it a couple of centuries older than the oldest of the Dead Sea Scrolls.

While the story is set during the Assyrian Captivity of the Samaritans during the 7th century BCE, it is generally accepted by scholars that the book was written in its current form in the 6th century BCE, during the Babylonian Captivity of the Judahites. The primary reason for this dating is the repeated referenced to Bỏlå (ﬡﬞ ﬥﬠﬦ), which is generally accepted as a reference to the Neo-Babylonian god of the 6th century BCE named Belu (-ﬗ), more commonly called Bel in English based on his appearance in the Septuagint's Book of

1

Daniel, where he was called Bel (Βῆλ). This book also repeatedly refers to the Highest God, El Elyon, the ancient Canaanite and Israelite god from the Torah, however, does not mention Yehwa, and therefore does not appear to have been written by a Judahite. As Tobit claimed to be Ahikar's uncle, and a Naphtalite captive in Assyria, this indicates that Ahikar was viewed as being a Samaritan, and not a Judahite at the time that Tobit was written.

While Bôlå (𐡍𐡋𐡏𐡉) was the Aramaic translation of Belu (-𒁹), it was also the Aramaic translation of the Canaanite term Bôl (𐤋𐤏𐤁), more commonly spelled as Ba'al in English based on the Hebrew spelling of ba'al (בַּעֲל), meaning 'lord,' or "husband." This means that if the text was written by a Samaritan during the Neo-Assyrian era, the term would have been a common Canaanite word used in Samaria for 'the Lord,' or at least a "Lord." According to all historical evidence, and the written evidence in the Septuagint and Masoretic Text, the Israelites at the time were using the term Ba'al to refer to several gods, including the god worshiped at the temples in Jerusalem and Samaria. Nevertheless, by the era of the oldest surviving fragments of Ahikar, the term does appear to have been interpreted as a reference to the Neo-Babylonian Bel, likely because the Israelites had stopped referring to their gods as Ba'al by that era.

Based on the Aramaic language Elephantine papyri, several Israelite deities were being worshiped at the Israelite Temple in Elephantine in the early 5ᵗʰ century BCE, including Yehwa, Anat, and Bethel. Bel does not appear to have been

2

worshiped at the temple at the time, meaning that the Words of Ahikar would have already been viewed as a somewhat heretical historical text, much like the early Rabbinical view of Daniel, Proverbs, Ecclesiastes, Ezekiel, Job, and Enoch. Nevertheless, as Elephantine was the southern frontier of the Persian Empire at the time, and the Israelite community had existed there for centuries, at least since the Babylonian destruction of Judah, and probably since the Assyrian destruction of Samaria, the text would have held a historical significance to the Israelites living there, regardless of which gods were in the book. Whoever Bel started out as, he was later translated out of the text to make it compatible with Christianity and Islam, replaced with 'the Lord' in Christian translations, and Allah in Islamic translations.

It does not appear to have been considered a religious book by Judahites under Greek rule, or later when Judea became independent, and was not included in either the Septuagint or the Masoretic Text. Nevertheless, the author of the Book of Tobit, which is in the Septuagint, clearly viewed the Words of Ahikar as authentic, as his protagonist Tobit claimed that he was Ahikar's uncle, and both Ahikar and his nephew Nadan make a brief appearance in the book of Tobit at Tobit's son Tobiah's marriage feast in Nineveh. The Book of Tobit was likely written in the Median Empire, and carried into Judea by the priest Tobiah, who was listed as one of the leaders of the Israelites that returned to Judea after Cyrus II (the Great) released the Judahites when he conquered Babylon. Tobiah was later rejected from the Second Temple priesthood, as he could not prove his linage as a Levite, which is consistent with the Tobiah in the book of Tobit, who was a Naphtalite. A Tobian priesthood was later reported in Moab during Persian and Greek rule, suggesting the Book of Tobit was in use in the region. The Tobian Judahites (Τουβιανοὺς Ιουδαίους) also appear to be the source of the Testaments of the Patriarchs, which for the most part were not accepted by the Sadducees and Pharisees, but were later adopted by the Christians, Sethians, and Gnostics.

The Words of Ahikar is not considered to be a true historical story by any modern academics or theologians. It is universally considered to be a work of fiction for several reasons, not the least of which are the boys flying on the back of trained eagles. Another reason that the work is not considered historical, is that the Assyrian kings are not mentioned in the correct order, as King Esarhaddon was actually Sennacherib's son, not his father. Both Kings are well known from the historical records of the Assyrians, Babylonians, and Egyptians. Moreover, Esarhaddon and his son Ashurbanipal liberated Egypt from Kushite rule, and established the vassal state of Egypt which ultimately became independent again when the Neo-Assyrian Empire fell. During the time of Sennacherib, Egypt was still under the control of Kush, and there was no Pharaoh for Ahikar to visit.

The book also refers to a King of Persia, centuries before there was a Kingdom of Persia, and is therefore generally dismissed as a work of historical-fiction. Nevertheless, the book of Tobit records that Ahikar was sent to Elam as an envoy, not Persia. As the Persians settled in the land of Elam after King Ashurbanipal destroyed Elam in the mid 7th century BCE, the name Persia would have been the contemporary geographical term when the Aramaic translation was made, and not the original term. In any event, the author of Tobit must have had a copy of Ahikar that used the name Elam instead of Persia, or his reference to Ahikar going to Elam makes no sense. As Ahikar, Tobit, and Tobiah are all reported as living in Nineveh under the reign of Esarhaddon, and both Tobit and Ahikar are reported to have worked in his court, they would have almost certainly written their books in Neo-Assyrian Cuneiform. Tobiah, Tobit's son added to Tobit's writing after he moved to Media, which would have probably also have been in Neo-Assyrian, and the earliest Aramaic translation of Tobit was probably not made until the Persian era, when the Median King Cyaxares (Αχιαχαροσ) was replaced with the Babylonian king Nebuchadnezzar (Ναβουχοδονοσορ) and the Persian king Xerxes (Ασυηροσ). This indicates that the Neo-Assyrian original of Ahikar used the name Elam, not Persia, and therefore is not evidence of the book being written later, during the Persian era.

Regardless of the obvious fictional additions to the text, there is some evidence supporting the existence of Ahikar as a historical person. A cuneiform text discovered in the ruins of Uruk in southern Iraq, mentions that Aḫuúkaari (𒈨𒐊𒈨𒐊𒈨𒐊) was the Akkadian name of the sage Aba Enlil Dari (𒈨𒐊 𒈨𒐊 𒈨𒐊) during the reign of the Assyrian King Esarhaddon. This correlates with the opening of Ahikar, where King Sennacherib claims that Ahikar had served his father Esarhaddon, unfortunately, Esarhaddon was actually Sennacherib's son, not his father. Therefore, one of the names of the kings must have been replaced at some point, either the elder king, called Esarhaddon in the surviving text, or the younger king, called Sennacherib in the text.

The historical succession of Assyrian kings who may have been in the original text were Sargon II, Sennacherib, Esarhaddon, and Ashurbanipal. Sargon II was the king that fought the Levantine Wars, and in the process destroyed Samaria. The conquest of Samaria took three years, and was finally completed in the first year of his successor Sennacherib. During the war, Sargon reported deporting 27,280 Samaritans, who were resettled in other regions of his empire. Sennacherib reported deporting more in the aftermath of the war. It seems unlikely that Ahikar could have worked for Sargon II, before or during the Levantine Wars, as he was clearly some kind of Canaanite, and probably a Samaritan as Tobit reported. Therefore, it is probable that elder king was named Esarhaddon, and the younger king was Ashurbanipal, the same king as in Tobit.

King Sennacherib continued Sargon's campaigns in Levant, including the siege of Jerusalem, and it seems unlikely that Ahikar would have been sent to the Empire of Kush to represent Assyrian interests while the Assyrians were at war against his own people, and the Kushites were backing them. Nevertheless, Sennacherib is a much more famous king in the Israelite scriptures compared to Ashurbanipal, who existed peacefully with his vassal King Manasseh of Judah, and was hardly mentioned. This may be the reason he was later replaced by Sennacherib, like the other kings who were replaced by more famous kings in the various versions of the books of Tobit, Judith, and Esther.

King Esarhaddon, the elder king in Ahikar, and the king he served according to the tablet found in Uruk, did not fight any recorded wars against Judah, as King Manasseh appears to have been a firm Assyrian-ally throughout his reign. Esarhaddon did fight a series of wars in the north, against the kingdom of Urartu in the Armenian highlands, and the Cimmerians from Ukraine, who launched a massive invasion of the western region of the Assyrian empire after defeating the kingdoms of western Anatolia. After his victory in the north, he turned his attention to the south and launched a massive invasion of the Kushite Empire, sacking northern Egypt in 671 BCE. In 669 BCE he launched another campaign into Kush, attempting to reach southern Egypt, but died en route to Egypt. It is unclear if he died of natural causes or was assassinated, as he did have poor health, and there were several assassination plots that were foiled in the latter years of his life.

King Ashurbanipal continued his father's campaigns in Egypt in 667 BCE, and managed to capture Thebes in southern Egypt, which they reorganized into a Persian tributary, placing King Necho I on the throne of Egypt, before withdrawing to Assyria, in 664 BCE. This withdrawal was immediately followed by the king of Kush invading Egypt, and killing Necho I. The Assyrians returned in force, and drove the Kushites from Egypt, placing Necho I's heir Psamtik I on the throne. This occupation of Thebes was recorded as the 'Sack of Thebes,' in the Assyrian and Israelite records. The Assyrians are believed to have taken over 75 tons of gold from Thebes, most of which had been coating the exterior of statues and obelisks. Both the Judahite prophet Isaiah, and the Babylonian prophet Nahum commented on this, with Nahum predicting that Assyria would one day suffer the same fate. At the time, Babylonia was quasi-independent under the rule of Ashurbanipal's elder brother Shamash-shum-ukin, and so criticism of Assyria appears to have been tolerated.

The exact level of Babylonian independence at the time is unclear, however, it appears that Esarhaddon placed his sons on the thrones of the two kingdoms of Assyria and Babylon in order to avoid a civil war after he died. Ashurbanipal was the more militant, and placed on the throne of Assyria to continue the wars against Egypt and Urartu, while Shamash-shum-ukin was placed on the throne of Babylon to continue rebuilding the nation that had been largely destroyed when the Assyrian king Tiglath-Pileser had captured it around a century earlier. Esarhaddon had invested significantly in rebuilding the land, and Shamash-shum-ukin continued his work for decades before openly declaring war against his brother Ashurbanipal who had tried to incorporate Babylonia into the Assyrian Empire. As the Assyrians ultimately won the war, this was recorded as a civil war in the Assyrian records, however, Babylonia appears to have been a functionally independent closely allied state under the rule of

Shamash-shum-ukin, with its own military and foreign relations.

Nahum's prophecy against Assyria is referenced in the Codex Sinaiticus' version of Tobit, however, it is substituted by Jonah's prophecy against Assyria in the Codex Vaticanus' version of Tobit. While the conflicting versions of Tobit may not be the best historical evidence for the existence of Ahikar, it is worth noting that Ahikar and his nephew Nadan are mentioned as attending Tobiah's wedding in Nineveh during the reign of Esarhaddon, which would have to have been before Nadan betrayed Ahikar. This, combined with the claim that Ahikar was the son of Tobit's brother Anael, and that they both served Esarhaddon, indicate that at least the author of Tobit believed that Ahikar served Esarhaddon and Ashurbanipal, not Sargon and Sennacherib.

The references to Bel in the oldest surviving copies of Ahikar indicate that the Aramaic translation was made in the Neo-Babylonian Empire, which explains why the name of Ashurbanipal would have been replaced, as he fought a massive war against Babylonia, and reoccupied it after defeating his brother Shamash-shum-ukin. No book about someone serving Ashurbanipal would have been popular in the Neo-Babylonian empire, and owning one could have been viewed as treason in and of itself after Babylon finally threw off the shackles of Assyria.

There are few other historic references to someone who may have been Ahikar, however, these references are generally centuries later, and may simply be based on people reading copies of the Words of Ahikar. In the 5th century BCE, the Greek historian Herodotus mentioned a similar character named "Croesus" (Κροῖσος), however, placed the wise sage in the court of the Persian King Cyrus I, around 50 years after the events described int the Words of Ahikar. Some modern historians believe that Croesus is a corruption of the Greek version of Ahikar's name: Aḱiaḱaros (Αχιαχαρος), making Herodotus' Croesus another version of the Ahikar story, however, the name Croesus is more commonly viewed as being derived from the Lydian name Krowiśaś (𐤓𐤀𐤓𐤉𐤕𐤏𐤔), making any connection between Ahikar and Croesus speculative. If Ahikar did serve in the court of Esarhaddon, which all copies of Ahikar and Tobit agree on, then he would have been an adult before Esarhaddon's death in 705 BCE, while King Cyrus I did not become king of Persia until 600 BCE, making this seem to be an impossibility. In the 1st century BCE, the Greek historian Strabo mentioned an ancient eastern sage named Aḱaikarus (Αχαικαρος), who many believe was a reference to Ahikar, however, Strabo could have simply read a copy of the Words of Ahikar.

The Words of Ahikar includes many similar sayings to the Septuagint's Book of Proverbs, which many interpret as being an Judahite influence, however, the Book of Proverbs could have also been used by Samaritans at the time. Other than the existence of El Elyon (the Highest God) there does not seem to be any common element with the Torah. There is no mention of Abraham, Issac, Jacob, Moses, Aaron, or Joshua, and therefore this book could be interpreted as a Canaanite work, and not Israelite at all, meaning neither Jewish nor Samaritan, however, it is generally assumed by academics to be Israelite. The surviving full copies in Greek, Armenian, and Arabic, all show signs of later Christian or Islamic editors, and therefore, it is unclear who wrote the book, a Canaanite or an Israelite, however, it does mention Bel by name, which is taken as proof that it was either written or edited in the Neo-Babylonian Empire, and it does mention El Elyon by name, which is taken as proof it is Israelite. This is in and of itself not conclusive, as the Arameans in northern Canaan are recorded as worshiping a version of El Elyon, called âl wâlyn (ᒐᐟ ᔭ^ᒐᐟᐅᐧ), in the Sfire Treaties of the mid 8th century BCE.

Unfortunately, while the fragments found in Elephantine do allow us to restore the name Bel to the text, which was changed to either "Lord" (κύριος), or Allah (الله) in surviving copies, the fragments do not indicate who the god was before the Neo-Babylonian Aramaic translation. Moreover as all surviving translations appear to be based on an Aramaic translation made in the Neo-Babylonian era, they all also include the anachronisms that the Aramaic translator introduced when he obfuscated King Ashurbanipal, creating a somewhat nonsensical text from the historical perspective. Therefore two versions are included in this translation. The first is a translation of the Words of Ahikar, reconstructed primarily from the Greek version, with comparisons to the Aramaic fragments, as well as the Arabic, Armenian, and Old Slavonic translations. The second version is a historical restoration that uses the name Ashurbanipal instead of Sennacherib, and corrects other anachronisms as much as possible. In both versions there are still references to unknown places and peoples, however, after 2700 years, it does seem likely that there would be.

CHAPTER 1

This is the story of Ahikar[1] the sage, vizier of King Sennacherib,[2] and of Ahikar's nephew Nadan.[3]

There was a vizier in the days of King Sennacherib, son of King Esarhaddon[4] of Nineveh in Assyria, a wise man named Ahikar. He had a great fortune and a great deal of property, and he was skillful, wise, a philosopher in knowledge, and opinionated in government. He had married sixty women and had built a mansion for each of them. Yet he had no child by any of these women who could be his heir. He was very sad on account of this, and one day he assembled the astrologers and the learned men and the wizards and explained to them his condition and the matter of his barrenness. They said to him, "Go, sacrifice to the gods and beg them, maybe they will provide you with a son."

He did as they told him and offered sacrifices to the idols, and prayed to them and begged them with requests. They did not answer him even one word. He went away sad and dejected, departing with a pain at his heart. He returned and implored the Highest God,[5] and believed, begging him with a burning in his heart, saying, "Highest God, creator of the skies and the earth, creator of all created things! I beg you to give me a son, that I may be consoled by him, and that he may be present in my home, and that he may close my eyes, and that he may bury me."

CHAPTER 1

Then there came to him a voice saying, "As you have relied first of all on carved statues, and have offered sacrifices to them, for this reason, you will remain childless your whole life. But adopt Nadan your sister's son, and make him your child and teach him what you've learned and your good breeding, and at your death, he will bury you."

Thereafter he took Nadan his sister's son, who was still an infant. He handed him over to eight wet-nurses, that they might suckle him and raise him. They raised him with good food and gentle training and silk clothing, and purple and crimson, and he was seated on couches of silk. When Nadan grew big and walked, shooting up like a tall cedar, he taught him good manners and writing and science and philosophy. After many days King Sennacherib looked at Ahikar and saw that he had grown very old, and he said to him, "My honored friend, the skillful, trustworthy, wise governor, my secretary, my vizier, my chancellor, and director. You have grown very old and weighted with years, and your departure from this world must be near. Tell me who will have a place in my service after you."

Ahikar said to him, "My lord, may you live forever! There is Nadan my sister's son, I have adopted him as my child. I have brought him up and taught him my wisdom and knowledge."

The king said to him, "Ahikar, bring him into my presence so I may see him, and if I find him suitable put him in your place, and you will go your way, to take a rest and to live the remainder of your life in sweet repose."

CHAPTER 1

Then Ahikar went and presented Nadan his sister's son. He paid homage and wished him power and honor. He looked at him and admired him and rejoiced in him and said to Ahikar, "Is this your son, Ahikar? I pray that God may preserve him. As you have served me and my father Esarhaddon so may this boy of your serve me and fulfill my desires, needs, and business, so that I may honor him and make him powerful for your sake."

Ahikar paid obeisance to the king and said to him, "May you live forever, my lord king! I ask you that you may be patient with my boy Nadan and forgive his mistakes, so he may serve you as it is fitting."

Then the king swore to him that he would make him the greatest of his favorites, and the most powerful of his friends and that he should be with him in all honor and respect. He kissed his hands and bid him farewell. He took Nadan, his sister's son with him and seated him in a parlor and set about teaching him night and day until he had filled him with wisdom and knowledge more than with bread and water.

CHAPTER 1 NOTES

1 Aramaic: Åḥyqr (אֲחִיקַר)
- Greek: Aḱiaḱaros (Αχιαχαρος)
- Armenian Xikar (Խիկար)
- Arabic: Hayqār (حَيْقَار)
- Old Slavonic: Akyrios (Акѵрїосъ)

15

CHAPTER 1

The variations of the name Ahikar transliterated into various translations of the book indicate that most copies were made from the Aramaic version of the book. The Codex Sinaiticus' Tobit, chapter 11 also includes a direct translation of the Aramaic name as Aǩikar (Αχικαρ), confirming that the Aramaic translation of *Tobit* used the same name for him.

2 Aramaic: Snhryb (𐤔𐤍𐤇𐤓𐤉𐤁)
- Greek: Sanacharibos (Σαναχάριβος)
- Armenian: Sinak'erib (Սինաքերիբ)
- Arabic: Snhāryb (سنحاريب)

King Sîn-ahhī-erība (𒀭𒌍𒉽𒈨𒌍) was the king of the Assyrian Empire between 705 and 681 BCE. While all surviving versions of the Words of Ahikar agree that it was Sennacherib, the actual successor to Esarhaddon was Ashurbanipal, indicating that the name of Ashurbanipal was redacted. The oldest copy of the book, an Aramaic copy that had been in use at the Israelite Temple of Elephantine used the name Bel where the later translations substituted "God" or "Lord," indicating that the Aramaic translation was created in the Neo-Babylonian Empire, explaining why Ashurbanipal's name was removed from the text. Ashurbanipal devastated Babylonia and Elam during the civil/international war against his brother Shamash-shum-ukin and his allies in Elam in the 640s BCE.

The Assyrians won the war, but at such a tremendous financial cost, and with such a loss of prestige, that Nabopolassar was able to lead another Babylonian revolt in the 620s BCE, a few years after Ashurbanipal's death. This rebellion drew in virtually all of Assyria's neighbors, and ultimately destroyed the Neo-Assyrian Empire, dividing its territory between the newly independent Neo-Babylonian Empire, Median Empire, Kingdom of Persia, and

16

CHAPTER 1

Scythian Confederation. When the Aramaic version of Ahikar was translated, Ashurbanipal would have been seen in a similar light to how Hitler was viewed after the Second World War, making his redaction from the text a necessity.

Ahikar could not have worked for Sennacherib, who was one of the Assyrian Kings that conquered his homeland of Samaria and exiled his people. Sennacherib would not have sent a Samaritan captive to represent him in negotiations in Egypt or Elam. The Book of Tobit recorded that both Tobit and Ahikar worked for Esarhaddon, however, Ahikar was Tobit's nephew, and therefore would have continued to work for Esarhaddon's successor Ashurbanipal. Unfortunately, all known copies of Ahikar are based on the Aramaic translation, and therefore include this anachronism.

3 Aramaic: Ndn (𐤍𐤃𐤍)

- Greek: Nadab (Ναβαδ)
- Armenian: Nadin (Նադին)
- Arabic: Nbāb (نباب)

Nadan's name is not standardized, and appears to have diverged during the Persian era. This translation uses the Aramaic variant of Ndn, which is probably the original, and certainly served as the source for the Armenian variant of Nadin. The Greek of Nabab and Arabic variant of Nbāb, probably reflect a Persian era Moabite reinterpretation within the Aramaic versions of Ahikar. Ndb (𐤍𐤃𐤁) was a Moabite word meaning 'willing,' and often used in religious context for one who is 'willing to serve a god,' such as the name Kmš-ndb (𐤊𐤌𐤔𐤍𐤃𐤁), a Moabite king who agreed to pay tribute to Assyria after Sennacherib's Levantine Wars.

4 Aramaic: Åsrḥdwn (𐤀𐤎𐤓𐤇𐤃𐤅𐤍)

- Greek: Esarhaddon (Εσαρχαδδών)

CHAPTER 1

- Arabic: Åsrhdwn (آسرحدون)

Aššur-aḫa-iddina, more commonly known as Esarhaddon from the Hebrew version of his name 'Ēsar-ḥaddōn (אֵסַר־חַדֹּן) was actually Sennacherib's son, not his father. Esarhaddon was the king of the Assyrian Empire between 681 and 669 BCE. He is famous for conquering Egypt and creating the largest Empire in Middle-eastern history until then.

5 The Highest is a reference to God, or a god, found in many ancient religions in the region. According to the Torah, the ancient people of Jerusalem worshiped 'ēl 'elyôn (אֵל עֶלְיוֹן), which translates as 'God highest' when Abraham passed through the region. The Greeks translated it as Ṯeō tō usistō (Θεω τω υψιστω) in the Septuagint, also meaning 'God the highest.' El elyon is known to have been a major god of the Canaanites, called ål wålyn (𐤉𐤏𐤋𐤍𐤉 𐤋𐤍), meaning "God and highest" in an Aramaic language Sefire Treaty from circa 750 BCE.

The Greek translations of Sanchuniathon's bronze age writing that have survived to the present, referred to the primordial creator god of the Canaanites as Elioun (Ελιουν), which appears to be the same god. According to Sanchuniathon, Elioun was the "highest" (υψιστος) god, who made the sky and the land, and they made the rest of the gods. While the many references to Bel in this text appear to refer to the Babylonian god Bel, these references to the Highest are clearly references to the old Canaanite god El elyon.

A version of El elyon was worshiped by the Neo-Assyrians in the form of [deity]Šar (𒀭𒊹), more commonly called Anshar today. Anshar translates directly as 'deity totality' or 'deity eternity,' and was perceived in the later Neo-Assyrian era as the patriarch of the gods who created everything.

CHAPTER 2

He taught him, saying, "My son! Hear my speech and follow my advice and remember what I say.

My son, if you hear a word, let it remain in your heart, and don't reveal it to another, in case it becomes a lump of burning coal and burns your tongue and causes pain in your body, and you become reproachful and are shamed before God and man.

My son, if you have heard a report, don't spread it, and if you have seen something, don't tell it.

My son, make your speech easy to the listener and do not rush to answer questions.

My son, when you have heard anything, don't hide it.

My son, don't loosen a sealed knot, or untie it, and don't seal a loosened knot.

My son, don't covet outward beauty, for it fades and passes away, but instead an honorable memory that lasts forever.

My son, don't let a foolish woman deceive you with her speech, in case you die the most miserable of deaths, and she entangles you in a net until you are trapped.

My son, don't desire a woman beautified with clothing and with ointments, who is despicable and foolish in her mind. Woe to you if you bestow on her anything that is yours or commit to her what is in your hand and she entices you into sin, and God becomes angry with you.

My son, do not be like the almond-tree, for it brings out leaves before all the trees, and edible fruit after them all, but be like the mulberry-tree, which brings out edible fruit before all the trees, and leaves after them all.

My son, bend your head low down, and soften your voice, and be courteous, and walk in the straight path, and don't be foolish. Don't raise your voice when you laugh for if it were by a loud voice that a house was built, the donkey would build many houses every day, and if it were just through strength that the plow was driven, the plow would never be removed from under the shoulders of the camels.

My son, the moving of stones with a wise man is better than the drinking of wine with a foolish man.

My son, pour out your wine on the tombs of the just and don't drink with ignorant, contemptible people.

My son, cling to wise men who fear God and be like them, and don't go near the ignorant, in case you become like him and learn his ways.

My son, when you have a comrade or a friend, test him, and afterward make him a comrade and a friend, and do not praise him without testing him. Do not waste your speech with a man who lacks wisdom.

My son, while a shoe stays on your foot, walk with it on the thorns, and make a road for your son, and for your household and your children, and make your ship taut before she goes on the sea and its waves and sinks and cannot be saved.

My son, if the rich man eats a snake, they say, "It is through his wisdom," and if a poor man eats it, the people say, "Because he is hungry."

My son, be content with your daily bread and your goods and don't covet what is another's.

My son, don't be neighbor to the fool, and don't eat bread with him, and don't rejoice in the calamities of your neighbors. If your enemy wrongs you, show him kindness.

My son, a man who fears God, fears him and honors him.

My son, the ignorant man falls and stumbles, and the wise man, even if he stumbles is not shaken, and even if he falls, he gets up quickly, and if he is sick he can take care of his life. But as for the ignorant, stupid man, there is no drug for his disease.

My son, if a man approaches you who is inferior to yourself, go forward to meet him and remain on your feet. If he cannot repay you, his lord will repay you for him.

My son, don't spare beating your son, for the beating of your son is like manure to the garden, and like tying the opening of a purse, and like the tethering of beasts, and like the bolting of the door.

My son, restrain your son from wickedness, and teach him manners before he rebels against you and brings you into contempt among the people and you hang your head in the streets and the assemblies and you be punished for the evil of his wicked deeds.

My son, get a fat ox with a foreskin, and a donkey with great hoofs, and don't get an ox with large horns, or make friends with a deceitful man, or get a quarrelsome slave, or a thievish handmaid, for everything which you give to them they will ruin.

My son, don't let your parents curse you, and the Lord[1] be pleased with them, for it has been said, "He who despises his father or his mother, let him die the death and he who honors his parents will prolong his days and his life and will see all that is good."

My son, don't travel the road without weapons, for you don't know when a foe may meet you, and you should be ready for him.

My son, do not be like a bare, leafless tree that does not grow, but be like a tree covered with its leaves and its boughs, for the man who has neither wife nor children is disgraced in the world and is hated by them, like a leafless and fruitless tree.

My son, be like a fruitful tree on the roadside, whose fruit is eaten by all who pass by, and the beasts of the desert rest under its shade and eat of its leaves.

My son, every sheep that wanders from its path and its companions becomes food for the wolf.

CHAPTER 2

My son, don't say, "My lord is a fool and I am wise," and don't relate the speech of ignorance and folly, in case you become hated by him.

My son, don't be one of those servants, to who their lords say, "Get away from us," but be one of those to whom they say, "Approach and come near to us."

My son, don't caress your slave in the presence of his companion, for you don't know which of them will be of most value to you in the end.

My son, don't be afraid of the Lord who created you, in case he is silent to you.

My son, make your speech fair and sweeten your tongue, and don't let your companion step on your foot, in case at another time he steps on your chest.

My son, if you defeat a wise man with a word of wisdom, it will lurk in his chest like a subtle sense of shame, but if you beat the ignorant with a stick he will neither understand nor hear.

My son, if you send a wise man for your needs, do not give him many orders, for he will do your business as you desire, and if you send a fool, do not order him, but go yourself and do your business, for if you order him, he will not do what you desire. If they send you on business, hurry to fulfill it quickly.

CHAPTER 2

My son, don't make an enemy of a man stronger than yourself, for he will take your measure, and his revenge on you.

My son, test your son, and your servant, before you trust your belongings to them, in case they run away with them, for he who has a full hand is called wise, even if he is stupid and ignorant, and he who has an empty hand is called poor and ignorant, even if he is the prince of sages.

My son, I have eaten colocynth,[2] and swallowed bitters, and I have found nothing more bitter than poverty and scarcity.

My son, teach your son frugality and hunger, that he may do well in the management of his household.

My son, don't teach the ignorant the language of wise men, for it will be burdensome to him.

My son, don't display your condition to your friend, in case you become despised by him.

My son, the blindness of the heart is more terrible than the blindness of the eyes, for the blindness of the eyes may be guided little by little, but the blindness of the heart is not guided, and it leaves the straight path and goes in a crooked way.

My son, the stumbling of a man with his foot is better than the stumbling of a man with his tongue.

My son, a friend who is near is better than a more excellent brother who is far away.

CHAPTER 2

My son, beauty fades but learning lasts, and the world fades and becomes vain, but a good name neither becomes vain nor fades.

My son, for the man who has no peace, his death is better than his life, and the sound of mourning is better than the sound of singing. If the fear of God is in them, sorrow and weeping are better than the sound of singing and rejoicing.

My child, the leg of a frog in your hand is better than a goose in the pot of your neighbor, and a sheep near you is better than an ox far away, and a sparrow in your hand is better than a thousand sparrows flying. Poverty which gathers is better than the scattering of many provisions, and a living fox is better than a dead lion. A pound of wool is better than a pound of gold or silver, for the gold and the silver are hidden and covered up in the earth and are not seen, but the wool stays in the markets and it is seen, and it is a beauty to him who wears it.

My son, a small fortune is better than a scattered fortune.

My son, a living dog is better than a dead poor man.

My son, a poor man who does right is better than a rich man who is dead because of his sins.

My son, keep a word in your heart, and it will be much to you and beware that you don't reveal the secret of your friend.

My son, don't let a word issue from your mouth until you have taken counsel with your heart. Stand not between quarreling people, because from an insult there comes a quarrel, and from a quarrel there comes a dispute, and from dispute there comes fighting, and you will be forced to bear witness. Instead, run from there and have peace.

My son, don't struggle with a man stronger than yourself, but have a patient spirit, and endure in upright conduct, for there is nothing more excellent than that.

My son, don't hate your first friend, for the second one may not last.

My son, visit the poor in his affliction, and speak of him in the king's presence, and do your diligence to save him from the mouth of the lion.

My son, don't rejoice in the death of your enemy, for after a little while you will be his neighbor, and he who mocks you, you respect and honor and greeting him first.

My son, if water would stand still in the sky, and a black crow become white, and myrrh grows sweet as honey, then ignorant men and fools might understand and become wise.

My son, if you desire to be wise, restrain your tongue from lying, and your hand from stealing, and your eyes from seeing evil, and then you will be called wise.

My son, let the wise man beat you with a wand but don't let the fool anoint you with sweet salve. Be humble in your youth and you will be honored in your old age.

My son, don't stand against a man in the days of his power, or a river in the days of its flood.

CHAPTER 2

My son, do not rush to wed a wife, for if it turns out well, she will say, "My lord, make provision for me," and if it turns out poorly, she will accuse him who was the cause of it.

My son, whoever is elegant in his dress, he is the same in his speech, and he who has a mean appearance in his dress, he also is the same in his speech.

My son, if you have committed a theft, make it known to the king, and give him a share of it, that you may be delivered from him, for otherwise, you will endure bitterness.

My son, make a friend of the man whose hand is satisfied and filled and don't make friends with the man whose hand is closed and hungry.

There are four things in which neither the king nor his army can be secure: oppression by the vizier, bad government, perversion of the will, and tyranny over the subjects, and four things which cannot be hidden: the prudent, the foolish, the rich, and the poor."

CHAPTER 2 NOTES

1 Aramaic: Bôlȧ (ܐܠ݂ܥ). Translation: Bel (or Ba'al, Lord)
• Greek: Kurios (Κύριος). Translation: lord
• Armenian: Ter (Տէր). Translation: owner (or lord, master)
• Arabic: āllh (الله). Translation: god
• Old Slavonic: Gospodĭ (ᎶᏛᎡᏠᏛᏋ). Translation: lord (or master)

Chapter 2

The various later translations indicate that the Christian and/or Islamic God is being referred to, however, scholars believe the Aramaic version was referring to Bel, the supreme god of the Neo-Babylonian pantheon. If this analysis is correct, it means the Neo-Assyrian Cuneiform text of Ahikar must have been translated into Aramaic in the Neo-Babylonian Empire, which supports the removal of the name of Ashurbanipal. Bel was worshiped by the Babylonians in the first millennium BCE. He was a syncretization of the older Mesopotamian Marduk, Enlil, and Dumuzid. However, his name simply translates as "Lord," meaning that Ahikar could have simply been using the term 'Lord.'

Whichever god Ahikar was referring to, if he was living in Assyria under Ashurbanipal, he would not have been worshiping the god of the renegade Neo-Babylonians, meaning that Bel can only be accepted as the original god in the text if it is assumed that Ahikar did not exist, and the book is a work of fiction, written in the Neo-Babylonian era. However, this also seems improbable, as a book about a Samaritan worshiper of Bel living in the Neo-Assyrian Empire, should anyone decide to write something so obscure, would have been written in Neo-Babylonian Cuneiform, and probably not translated into Aramaic until the Persian era, resulting in the reading of "Bel" being erased by the Israelites abandoning the title Ba'al for their god during the Neo-Babylonian era in response Bel being the supreme god of the people who destroyed Jerusalem. As the setting of the book is Assyria, not Babylonia, the Assyrian reading of Belu (-𒂗) is used in this translation, generally rendering the term as "Lord," as it appears in Greek, Aramaic, and Old Slavonic translations.

There are specific references to an Idol of Bel / Lord / Allah, however, as there was no known statue at the time of the Lord or Allah, the translation of Bel is used, however, it is unlikely Bel was originally in the Neo-Assyrian text. The references to the Idol of

28

CHAPTER 2

Bel, take place in 'Egypt,' which may have been Kush at the time when Ahikar was speaking to the Pharaoh, indicating that the author was referring to an Egyptian or Kushite god, not a Babylonian god. As the name of the god is no longer in any of the texts, the reference to Bel is used in relation to the idol.

2   Colocynth, also called bitter apples, is a vine native to the Mediterranean region and was once cultivated across Anatolia, the Middle East, Egypt, and Kush. It was cultivated in Egypt since pre-Dynastic times, since at least 3800 BCE. By the classical era, it was mainly used for medicine. Today it is primarily cultivated for medicine or bio-fuel.

CHAPTER 3

So spoke Ahikar, and when he had finished these injunctions and proverbs to Nadan, his sister's son, he imagined that he would keep them all, and he did not know that instead, that he was seeing him as weary and contemptible, and mocking him. Ahikar sat in his house afterward and gave to Nadan all his goods, and the slaves, and the handmaidens, and the horses, and the livestock, and everything else that he had possessed and gained, and the power of bidding and of forbidding was given to the hand of Nadan. Ahikar sat in peace in his house, and occasionally Ahikar went and paid his respects to the king, and returned home.

When Nadan saw that the power of bidding and forbidding was in his hands, he despised the position of Ahikar and scoffed at him, and set about blaming him whenever he appeared, saying, "My uncle Ahikar is in his old age, and he knows nothing anymore."

He began to beat the slaves and the handmaidens and to sell the horses and the camels and he spent all that his uncle Ahikar had owned. When Ahikar saw that he had no compassion on his servants or his household, he arose and chased him from his house, and sent a message to inform the king that he had scattered his possessions and his provision.

The king arose and called Nadan and said to him, "While Ahikar remains in health, no one will rule his goods, or his household, or over his possessions."

The hand of Nadan was lifted off from his uncle Ahikar and all his goods, and in the meantime, he neither went in or out nor did he greet him. Afterward, Ahikar regretted the struggle with Nadan his sister's son, and he continued to be very sad. Nadan had a younger brother named Benuzardan, so Ahikar took him for himself instead of Nadan, and raised him and honored him with the greatest honors. He gave over to him all that he possessed and made him ruler of his house.

Now when Nadan found out what had happened he was seized with envy and jealousy, and he began to complain to everyone who questioned him, and to mock his, uncle Ahikar, saying, "My uncle has chased me from his house and has preferred my brother to me, but if the Highest God gives me the power, I will cause him to be killed."

Nadan thought about what trap he might set for him. After a while, Nadan turned it over in his mind and wrote a letter to Achish,[1] son of King Wise,[2] the king of Persia,[3] saying:

"Peace and health and strength and honor from Sennacherib, king of Nineveh in Assyria, and from his vizier and his secretary Ahikar to you, great king! Let there be peace between you and me.

When this letter reaches you, if you will rise and go quickly to the plains of the protectors,[4] and to Nineveh in Assyria, I will deliver up the kingdom to you with-

out war and without a battle-formation."

He wrote also another letter in the name of Ahikar to Pharaoh king of Egypt:[5]

"Let there be peace between you and me, mighty king!

If at the time when this letter reaches you, you rise and go to Nineveh in Assyria to the plain of the protectors, I will deliver up to you the kingdom without war and without fighting."

The letters of Nadan looked like the letters of his uncle Ahikar. He folded the two letters and sealed them with the seal of his uncle Ahikar, and they were left in the king's palace. Then he went and wrote a similar letter from the king to his uncle Ahikar:

"Peace and health to my vizier, my secretary, my chancellor, Ahikar,

Ahikar, when this letter reaches you, assemble all the soldiers who are with you, and let them be in perfect clothing and in great numbers, and bring them to me on the fifth day in the plain of the protectors.

When you see me there coming towards you, quickly have the army move against me like an enemy who would fight with me, for I have with me the ambassadors of Pharaoh king of Egypt, that they may see the strength of our army and may fear us, for they are our enemies and they hate us."

Then he sealed the letter and sent it to Ahikar by one of the king's servants. He took the other letter which he had written and spread it before the king and read it to him and showed him the seal. When the king heard what was in the letter he was perplexed and greatly confused and fiercely angry, and said, "Oh, I have been shown wisdom! What have I done to Ahikar that he has written these letters to my enemies? Is this my repayment for my gifts to him?'

Nadan said to him, "Do not be sad, king! Nor be angry, but let us go to the plain of the protectors and see if the story is true or not."

Then Nadan arose on the fifth day and took the king and the soldiers and the vizier, and they went to the desert to the plain of the protectors. The king looked and saw Ahikar and the army set in formation. When Ahikar saw that the king was there, he approached and signaled to the army to move as they would in war and to fight in formation against the king as it had been told in the letter, not knowing the trap Nadan had set for him.

When the king saw the acts of Ahikar he was seized with anxiety and terror and confusion and was very angry. Nadan said to him, "Have you seen, my lord the king, what this wretch has done? Do not be angry and do not be sad or hurt, but go to your house and sit on your throne, and I will bring Ahikar to you bound and chained with chains, and I will chase away your enemy from before you without a battle."

CHAPTER 3

The king returned to his throne, being provoked about Ahikar, and did nothing about him. Nadan went to Ahikar and said to him, "Hello, my uncle! The king is very happy with you, and thanks you for having done what he commanded you. Now he has sent me to you that you may dismiss the soldiers to their duties and come yourself to him with your hands bound behind you, and your feet chained, that the ambassadors of Pharaoh may see this and that the king may be feared by them and by their king."

Then Ahikar answered, "To hear is to obey."

He arose right away and bound his hands behind him, and chained his feet, and Nadan took him to the king. When Ahikar entered the king's presence he did obeisance before him on the ground and wished for power and perpetual life to the king. Then the king demanded, "Ahikar, my secretary, the governor of my affairs, my chancellor, the ruler of my state, tell me what evil have I done to you that you have rewarded me by this terrible deed."

Then they showed him the letters in his writing and with his seal. When Ahikar saw this, his limbs trembled and his tongue was tied at once, and he was unable to speak a word from fear, but he hung his head towards the earth and was dumb. When the king saw this, he felt certain that the scheme was from him, and he immediately rose and commanded them to execute Ahikar and to chop his neck with the sword outside of the city. Then Nadan screamed and said, "Ahikar! What makes you thing you can do things to the king?"

CHAPTER 3

(So says the story-teller.)

The name of the swordsman was Abi Samik. The king said to him, "Swordsman! Rise and go cut the neck of Ahikar at the door of his house, and throw away his head from his body a hundred cubits."

Then Ahikar knelt before the king, and said, "Let my lord the king live forever! If you desire to slay me, let your wish be fulfilled, and I know that I am not guilty, but the wicked man has to give an account of his wickedness, nevertheless, my lord the king, I beg of you and from your friendship, permit the swordsman to give my body to my slaves, that they may bury me, and let your slave be your sacrifice."

The king rose and commanded the swordsman to do with him according to his desire. He immediately commanded his servants to take Ahikar and the swordsman and take him naked, so they might slay him. When Ahikar knew for certain that he was to be slain he sent a message to his wife, and said to her, "Come out and meet me, and let there be with you a thousand young virgins, and dress them in gowns of purple and silk that they may cry for me before my death. Prepare a table for the swordsman and his servants, and prepare plenty of wine, that they may drink."

She did all that he commanded her. She was very wise, clever, and prudent. She united all possible courtesy and learning. When the army of the king and the swordsman arrived, he found the table set in order, and the wine and the

36

luxurious viands, and they began eating and drinking till they were gorged and drunken.

Then Ahikar took the swordsman aside, separate from the company and said, "Abi Samik, do you not know that when Esarhaddon the king, the father of Sennacherib, wanted to kill you, I took you and hid you in a certain place until the king's anger subsided and he asked for you? When I brought you into his presence he rejoiced in you, and now remember the kindness I did you. I know that the king will be sorry about me and will be very angry about my execution."

"For I am not guilty, and it will happen when you present me before him in his palace, you will meet with great fortune, and know that Nadan my sister's son has deceived me and has done this terrible deed to me, and the king will repent of having killed me. I have a well in the garden of my house, and no one knows of it. Hide me in it with only my wife knowing. I have a slave in prison who deserves to be killed. Bring him out and dress him in my clothes, and command the servants when they are drunk to slay him. They will not know who it is they are killing. Throw away his head a hundred cubits from his body, and give his body to my slaves that they may bury it. You have laid up a great treasure with me."

Then the swordsman did as Ahikar had commanded him, and he went to the king and said to him, "May you live forever!"

CHAPTER 3

Then each week, Ahikar's wife lowered down to him in his hiding-place everything he needed, and no one else knew of it. The story was reported and repeated and spread abroad in every place of how Ahikar the Sage had been slain and was dead, and all the people of that city mourned for him. They wept and said, "Alas for you, Ahikar, and for your learning and your courtesy! How sad it is to lose you and your knowledge! Where can another like you be found? Where can there be a man so intelligent, learned, and skilled in ruling as to resemble you that he may fill your place?"

The king repented killing Ahikar, but his repentance did not help him. Then he called for Nadan and said to him, "Go, and take your friends with you, and mourn and cry for your uncle Ahikar, and lament for him as is the custom, honoring in his memory."

But when Nadan, the foolish, the ignorant, the hardhearted, went to the house of his uncle, he neither wept nor mourned nor wailed, but assembled heartless and dissolute people and set about eating and drinking. Nadan began to seize the woman-slaves and the men-slaves belonging to Ahikar, and bound them and tortured them and beat them severely. He did not respect the wife of his uncle, she who had brought him up like her own son, but wanted her to sin with him. Ahikar had been in the hiding-place, and he heard the weeping of his slaves and his neighbors, and he praised the Highest God, the Merciful One, and gave thanks, and he continued to pray and implore the Highest God.

CHAPTER 3

The swordsman came from time to time to Ahikar while he was in the hiding-place, and Ahikar came and begged him. He comforted him and wished him deliverance. When the story was reported in other countries that Ahikar the Sage had been murdered, all the kings were sad and hated king Sennacherib, and they lamented over Ahikar the solver of riddles.

CHAPTER 3 NOTES

1 Aramaic: Åkẏš (𐡅𐡀𐡉𐡍)
- Greek: Akǩous (Ακχους)
- Armenian: Akhis (Ախիս)
- Arabic: Åḫyš (أخيش)

While the text refers to this as the son of "King Wise of Persia," it is likely that this began as a reference the Aramean chieftain Bel-Iqisha, who led an Elamite backed rebellion in southern Babylonian in 665 BCE. Åkẏš (𐡔𐡊𐡉𐡀) was also a popular Canaanite name at the time, and several Philistine kings bore the name, which was recorded in Neo-Assyrian Cuneiform as Ikaúsu (𒄿𒅗𒌑𒋢).

2 All translations refer to a "King Wise," however, there are no records of any Persian king named any variation of the word 'wise,' and at Persia did not exist as a kingdom at the time, this was probably a mistranslation of the name of the Elamite king Teumman, who backed the rebellion of Bel-Iqisha in 664 BCE. Teumman's name was virtually the same as the Babylonian word tēmānu (𒋼𒊬), which meant 'wise,' suggesting that the original

Neo-Assyrian story was about King Teumman and his proxy Bel-Iqisha.

3 All translations that survive to the present refer to this land as Persia, however, the Book of Tobit refers to it as Elam. This suggests that the term Persia was used in the original Aramaic translation made in the Neo-Babylonian Empire, which appears to have served for all later translations. This is historically valid, as Persia became a kingdom during the Neo-Babylonian era, and Elam no longer existed by the time that Babylon and its allies overthrew Assyria.

4 The word Nisrin, appear to be a Persian era reinterpretation of the older Neo-Assyrian cuneiform word naṣārum (𒀀𒌋𒐊𒈨). The Persian word nasrin (نسرین) means roses, while the Akkadian word meant 'protectors.' As the described geography places the Plain of Roses/Protectors in the region around Nineveh, and the Assyrians spoke Assyrian, and not Persian, the original meaning is restored.

5 All translations agree that this was Egypt, which if the previous references were to Bel-Iqisha and King Teumman in 664 BCE, would make this the first regal year of Pharaoh Wahibre Psamtik I, however, at the beginning of his reign he did not control Egypt, as the Kushites had invaded and captured most of the country, and in the process killed his predecessor Pharaoh Necho I. If Nadan had sent a letter to the king of Egypt at the time it would have been King Tantamani of Kush, who was at war against Assyria. The following year, 663 BCE, the Assyrian army reinvaded Egypt and drove out the Kushites, and spent the next few years occupying southern Egypt, meaning it could not have been later than 664 BCE.

40

CHAPTER 4

When the king of Egypt[1] had heard that Ahikar was dead, he rose immediately and wrote a letter to King Sennacherib, saying:

> *"Peace, health, might, and honor which we wish especially for you, my beloved brother, king Sennacherib.*
>
> *I have been desiring to build a castle in the air between the sky and the earth, and I want you to send me a wise, clever man from yourself to build it for me, and to answer me all my questions, and that I may have the tribute and the custom duties of Assyria for three years."*

Then he sealed the letter and sent it to Sennacherib, who took it and read it and gave it to his viziers and to the nobles of his kingdom, and they were confused and ashamed. He was very angry and was puzzled about how he should act. Then he assembled the old men and the learned men and the wise men and the philosophers, and the diviners and the astrologers, and everyone who was in his country, and read them the letter and said to them, "Who among you will go to Pharaoh king of Egypt and answer his riddles?"

They answered him, "Our lord king, you know that there is none in your kingdom who is acquainted with these riddles except Ahikar, your vizier and secretary. But as for us, we have no skill in this, unless it is Nadan, his sister's son, for he taught him all his wisdom and learning and knowledge. Call him to you, maybe he may untie this difficult knot."

Then the king called Nadan and said to him, "Look at this letter and understand what is in it."

When Nadan read it, he said, "My lord, who is able to build a castle in the air between the sky and the earth?"

When the king heard the question of Nadan he was very sad, and climbed down from his throne and sat in the ashes, and began to cry and wail over Ahikar saying, "My grief! Ahikar, who knew the secrets and the riddles! Woe to me, Ahikar! Teacher of my country and ruler of my kingdom, where will I find another like you? Ahikar, teacher of my country, where will I turn for you? Woe to me over you! How could I destroy you, and I listened to the talk of a stupid, ignorant boy without knowledge, without religion, without manliness. Why, and why again? Who can give you to me just for once, or bring me word that Ahikar is alive? I would give him half of my kingdom! What is this to me? Oh, Ahikar! That I might see you just once more. Oh! My grief for you, for all time! Ahikar, why have I killed you, and did not delay your case until I had seen all the information?"

The king went on weeping night and day, and when the swordsman saw the anger of the king and his sorrow for Ahikar, his heart was softened towards him, and he entered into his presence and said to him, "My lord! Command your servants to cut off my head."

CHAPTER 4

Then the king asked him, "Why Abi Samik, what is your fault?"

The swordsman said to him, "My master! Every slave who acts contrary to the word of his master is killed, and I have acted contrary to your command."

Then the king asked him, "Why Abi Samik? In what way have you disobeyed my command?"

The swordsman answered him, "My lord! You commanded me to kill Ahikar, and I knew that you would have regret concerning him and that he had been wronged, and I hid him in a certain place, and I killed one of his slaves, and he is now safe in the well, and if you command me I will bring him to you."

The king said to him, "Shame on you, Abi Samik! You are mocking me and I am your lord."

The swordsman replied to him, "No, but by your life, my lord! Ahikar is safe and alive."

When the king heard this, he felt sure of the matter, and his head swam, and he fainted from joy. He commanded them to bring Ahikar. He said to the swordsman, "Trusty servant! If your words are true, I will greatly enrich you, and praise you above all your friends."

The swordsman went out rejoicing and traveled to Ahikar's house. He opened the door of the hiding-place, and went down and found Ahikar sitting, praising God, and

43

thanking him. He called to him, saying, "Ahikar, I bring the greatest of joy, and happiness, and delight!"

Ahikar asked him, "What is the news, Abi Samik?"

He told him all about Pharaoh from the beginning to the end. Then he took him and went to the king. When the king looked at him, he saw him in a state of need, and that his hair had grown long like the wild beasts' and his nails were like the claws of an eagle, and that his body was dirty with dust, and the color of his face had changed and faded and was now like ashes. When the king saw him he was sad because of him and rose at once and embraced him and kissed him, and wept over him and said, "Praise the god who has brought you back to me."

Then he consoled him and comforted him. He stripped off his robe, and put it on the swordsman, and was very gracious to him, and gave him great wealth, and gave Ahikar peace. Then Ahikar said to the king, "Let my lord the king live forever! These are the deeds of the children of the world. I have raised a palm-tree that I might lean on it, and it bent sideways and threw me down. My lord, since I have appeared before you, don't let concerns oppress you!"

The king said to him, "Blessed is the god, who showed you mercy, and knew that you were wronged, and saved you and delivered you from being slain. Go to the warm bath, and shave your head, and cut your nails, and change your clothes, and amuse yourself for forty days, that you may be good to yourself and improve your condition and the color of your face may come back to you."

Then the king stripped off his costly robe and put it on Ahikar, and Ahikar thanked God and did obeisance to the king, and departed to his house glad and happy, praising the Highest God. The people of his household rejoiced with him, and his friends and everyone who heard that he was alive rejoiced also.

CHAPTER 4 NOTES

1 Assuming that the original Assyrian king in the story was Ashurbanipal, then this would have to be King Psamtik I, who ruled Egypt from 663 BCE, when Ashurbanipal placed him on the throne of Egypt as an Assyrian vassal to 610 BCE, several decades after the fall of Assyria. There are no surviving records of him attempting to build a castle in the sky, or anything else of significance. Most of his reign seems to have been focused on military campaigns and politics. He managed to defend Egypt from any further Kushite incursions, and successfully transitioned the country from being an Assyrian vassal to an independent nation. After Assyria fell, he spent the next few couple of decades competing with the Babylonians for control of Canaan.

CHAPTER 5

He did as the king commanded him, and rested for forty days. Then he dressed himself in his nicest clothes, and rode to the king, with his slaves behind him and before him, rejoicing and delighted. But when Nadan saw what was happening, fear took hold of him and terror, and he was confused, not knowing what to do.

When Ahikar saw it he entered into the king's presence and greeted him, and he returned the greeting, and made him sit down at his side, saying to him, "My friend Ahikar! Look at these letters which the king of Egypt sent to us after he heard that you were killed. They have provoked us and confused us, and many of the people of our country have fled to Egypt in fear of the tribute that the king of Egypt has demanded from us."

Then Ahikar took the letter and read it, and understood its contents. Then he said to the king, "Do not be angry, my lord! I will go to Egypt, and I will return the answers to Pharaoh, and I will display this letter to him, and I will reply to him about the tribute, and I will send back all those who have run away, and I will put your enemies to shame with the help of the Highest God, and for the happiness of your kingdom."

When the king heard this speech from Ahikar he rejoiced greatly, and his heart was expanded and he showed him favor. Ahikar asked the king, "Grant me a delay of forty days that I may consider this question and answer it."

The king permitted this, and Ahikar returned to his home. He commanded the hunters to capture two young eagles for him, and they captured them and brought them to him. He commanded the weavers of ropes to weave two cotton ropes for him, each two thousand cubits long. He had the carpenters brought to him and ordered them to make two great boxes, which they did. Then he took two young boys, and spent every day sacrificing lambs, and feeding the eagles and the boys. He made the boys ride on the backs of the eagles, and he bound them with a firm knot, and tied the cable to the feet of the eagles, and let them soar upwards little by little every day, to a distance of ten cubits, until they grew used to it and were trained to do it. They rose all the length of the rope until they reached the sky, with the boys on their backs. Then he pulled them back to himself.

When Ahikar saw that his plan was working he ordered the boys that when they were carried up into the sky, they were to shout, "Bring us clay and stone, so we can build a castle for king Pharaoh, as we are idle."

Ahikar was never done training them and exercising them until they had reached the highest possible place. Then leaving them he went to the king and said to him, "My lord! The work is finished as to your desire. Rise with me that I may show you the wonder."

CHAPTER 5

So the king got up and sat with Ahikar and went to a wide place and sent to bring the eagles and the boys, and Ahikar tied them and let them up into the air all the length of the ropes, and they began to shout as he had taught them. Then he drew them to himself and put them in their places. The king and those who were with him wondered greatly, and the king kissed Ahikar between his eyes and said to him, "Go in peace, my friend, pride of my kingdom, to Egypt and answer the riddles of Pharaoh and overcome him by the strength of the Highest God."

Then he commanded him farewell, and took his troops and his army and the young men and the eagles, and went towards the dwellings of Egypt, and when he had arrived, he turned towards the country of the king.

When the people of Egypt knew that Sennacherib had sent a man of his trusted council to talk with Pharaoh and to answer his questions, they took the news to king Pharaoh, and he sent a party of his trusted councilors to bring him before him.

He came and entered into the presence of Pharaoh, and did obeisance to him as it is fitting to do to kings, and he said to him, "My lord the king, Sennacherib the king hails you with abundance of peace and might, and honor. He has sent me, who is one of his servants, that I may answer you your questions, and may fulfill all your desire, for you have sent a message to my lord the king seeking a man who will build you a castle between the sky and the earth. I, through the help of the Highest God and your noble favor and the power

49

of my lord the king will build it for you as you desire. But, my lord king, what you have said about the tribute of Egypt for three years, now the stability of a kingdom is strict justice, and if you win and my hand has no skill in replying to you, then my lord the king will send you the tribute which you have mentioned. If I will have answered you in your questions, it will remain for you to send whatever you have mentioned to my lord the king."

When Pharaoh heard that speech, he wondered and was perplexed by the freedom of his tongue and the pleasantness of his speech. King Pharaoh asked him, "Man, what is your name?"

He answered, "Your servant is Abi Qam, and I am but a little ant among the ants of King Sennacherib."

Pharaoh said to him, "Has your lord no one of higher dignity than you, that he has sent me a little ant to reply to me, and to talk with me?"

Ahikar said to him, "My lord king! I will pray to God Highest that I may fulfill what is on your mind, for God is with the weak that he may confound the strong."

Then Pharaoh commanded that they should prepare a living place for Abi Qam and supply him with provisions, meat, and drink, and all that he needed. When it was finished, three days afterward Pharaoh clothed himself in purple and red and sat on his throne, and all his viziers and the magnates of his kingdom were standing with their hands crossed, their feet close together, and their heads bowed.

CHAPTER 5

Pharaoh sent to fetch Abi Qam, and when he was presented to him, he did obeisance before him, and kissed the ground in front of him. King Pharaoh asked him, "Abi Qam, who am I like? And the nobles of my kingdom, who are they like?"

Ahikar answered him, "My lord king, you are like the god Bel, and the nobles of your kingdom are like his servants."

He said to him, "Go, and come back here tomorrow."

So Ahikar left as king Pharaoh had commanded him. In the morning, Ahikar returned into the presence of Pharaoh, and did obeisance, and stood before the king. Pharaoh was dressed in a red, and the nobles were dressed in white. Pharaoh asked him, "Abi Qam, who am I like? And the nobles of my kingdom, who are they like?"

Ahikar answered him, "My lord, you are like the sun, and your servants are like its beams."

Pharaoh replied to him, "Go to your home, and return here tomorrow."

Then Pharaoh commanded his court to wear pure white, and Pharaoh was dressed like them and sat on his throne, and he commanded them to fetch Ahikar. He entered and sat down before him, and Pharaoh asked him, "Abi Qam, who am I like? And my nobles, who are they like?"

Abi Qam answered him, "My lord, you are like the moon, and your nobles are like the planets and the stars."

Pharaoh replied to him, "Go, and tomorrow return here."

CHAPTER 5

Then Pharaoh commanded his servants to wear robes of various colors, and Pharaoh wore a red velvet dress, and sat on his throne, and commanded them to bring in Abi Qam. He entered and did obeisance before him, and he asked, "Abi Qam, who am I like? And my armies, who are they like?"

He answered, "My lord, you are like the month of Parmoute,[1] and your armies are like its flowers."

When the king heard it he rejoiced greatly and said, "The first time you compared me to the idol Bel, and my nobles to his servants. The second time you compared me to the sun, and my nobles to the sunbeams. The third time you compared me to the moon, and my nobles to the planets and the stars. The fourth time you compared me to the month of Parmoute, and my nobles to its flowers. But now, Abi Qam, tell me, your lord King Sennacherib, who is he like? And his nobles, who are they like?"

Ahikar shouted with a loud voice and said, "It is far from me to make mention of my lord the king, while you are seated on your throne. Get up on your feet that I may tell you who my lord the king is like and who his nobles are like."

Pharaoh was confused by the freedom of his words and his boldness in answering. Pharaoh rose from his throne, and stood before Ahikar, and said, "Tell me now, that I may know who your lord the king is like, and who his nobles are like."

Ahikar said to him, "My lord is the sky god, and his nobles are the lightning and the thunder, and when he wills it, the winds blow and the rain falls. He commands the thunder, and

52

there is lightning and rain, and he holds the Sun, and it does not give its light, and the moon and the stars, and they don't circle. He commands the tempest, and it blows and the rain falls and it tramples in Parmoute and destroys its flowers and its houses."

When Pharaoh heard this speech, he was very confused and was extremely angry, and said to him, "Man, tell me the truth, and let me know who you really are."

He admitted the truth, "I am Ahikar the scribe, greatest of the trusted councilors of King Sennacherib, and I am his vizier and the governor of his kingdom, and his chancellor."

He said to him, "You have told the truth in this saying. But we have heard that king Sennacherib has executed Ahikar, yet you seem to be alive and well."

Ahikar answered him, "Yes, so it was, but praise be to God, who knows what is hidden, for my lord the king commanded me to be killed, and he believed the lies told of men, but the Lord saved me, and blessed is he who trusts in him."

Pharaoh said to Ahikar, "Go, and tomorrow return here, and tell me something that I have never heard from my nobles or the people of my kingdom and my country."

CHAPTER 5 NOTES

1 Greek: Farmouṯi (Φαρμουθί)
• Armenian: Pôarmutôi (Փարմուṫի)

CHAPTER 5

- Arabic: Baramūdah (برموده)

Pȧ-ĕn-rĕnĕn-wĕtĕt (𓂋𓈖𓏤𓃀𓏏) was the eighth month of the Egyptian civil calendar, and the last month of the Season of the "Emergence" (𓉔𓏏), when the Nile floods receded and the crops started to grow. It continued into the Coptic calendars as Parmoute (Παρμογτε) and Farmouṭi (Φαρμογѳι). This month is approximately April 9 to May 8 on the Gregorian calendar during the 21st century. It is generally translated as Parmoute in English from the Sahidic dialect of Coptic.

CHAPTER 6

Ahikar returned to his residence, and wrote a letter, saying in it on this:

"From King Sennacherib of Nineveh in Assyria to Pharaoh king of Egypt.

Peace be on you, my brother!

Let us make known to you through this message that a brother needs his brother, and kings of each other, and my hope from you is that you would lend me nine hundred talents of gold, for I need it for the provisioning of some of the soldiers, and I will spend it on them. At some point, I will return it to you."

Then he folded the letter and presented it in the morning to Pharaoh. When he saw it, he was confused and said to him, "I have never heard anything like these words from anyone."

Then Ahikar said to him, "Truly this is a debt which you owe to my lord the king."

Pharaoh accepted this, saying, "Ahikar, it is your way to be honest in the service of kings. Blessed be God who has made you perfect in wisdom and has adorned you with philosophy and knowledge. Now, Ahikar, there remains what we desire from you, that you should build as a castle between the sky and earth."

Then Ahikar replied, "To hear is to obey. I will build you a castle as you wish, but, my lord I will need lime, stone, clay, and workmen prepared. I have skilled builders who will build it for you as you desire."

The king prepared everything for him, and they went to a wide place where Ahikar also came, and he took the eagles and the young boys with him. The king and all his nobles went and the whole city assembled, that they might see what Ahikar would do. Then Ahikar let the eagles out of the boxes, and tied the young men on their backs, and tied the ropes to the eagles' feet, and let them go in the air. They soared upwards, till they were between the sky and earth. The boys began to shout, saying, "Bring bricks, bring clay, that we may build the king's castle, for we are standing idle!"

The crowd was astonished and perplexed, and they wondered. The king and his nobles wondered. Ahikar and his servants began to beat the workmen, and they shouted for the king's troops, saying to them, "Bring the skilled workmen what they want and do not stop them from their work."

The king said to him, "You are mad, who can bring anything up to that height?"

Ahikar said to him, "My lord, how will we build a castle in the air? If my lord the king were here, he would have built several castles in a single day."

Pharaoh said to him, "Leave Ahikar, to your residence, and rest. We have given up building the castle, but tomorrow return to me."

CHAPTER 6

Then Ahikar went to his residence and in the morning he returned to Pharaoh, and Pharaoh said, "Ahikar, what news is there of the horse of your lord? When he neighs in Nineveh in the country of Assyria, and our mares hear his voice, they abandon their young."

When Ahikar heard this riddle he went and took a cat, and tied her up and began to flog her violently until the Egyptians heard it, and they went and told the king about it. Pharaoh sent for Ahikar, and said to him, "Ahikar, why do you flog and beat that dumb animal?"

Ahikar said to him, my lord the king, she has done an ugly deed to me and has deserved this beating and flogging, for my lord King Sennacherib had given me a fine rooster, and he had a strong true voice and knew the hours of the day and the night. The cat got up this very night and bit off its head and went away, and because of this deed I have beaten her."

Pharaoh said to him, "Ahikar, I see from all this that you are growing old and are losing your mind, for between Egypt and Nineveh there are sixty-eight leagues,[1] and how did she go this very night and cut off the head of your rooster and returned?"

Ahikar said to him, "My lord, if there is such a distance between Egypt and Nineveh how could your mares hear when my lord the king's horse neighs and abandon their young? How could the voice of the horse reach Egypt?"

CHAPTER 6

When Pharaoh heard that, he knew that Ahikar had answered his riddle, and Pharaoh said, "Ahikar, I want you to make me ropes from the sea-sand."

Ahikar said to him, "My lord king, order them to bring me a rope out of the treasury that I may make one like it."

Then Ahikar went to the back of the house, and drilled holes in the rough shape of the sea, and took a handful of sand in his hand, sea-sand. When the sun rose and shone through the holes, he spread the sand in the sun till it looked like woven like ropes. Ahikar said, "Command your servants to take these ropes, and whenever you desire it, I will weave you some more like them."

Pharaoh said, "Ahikar, we have a millstone here and it has been broken and I want you to sew it up."

Then Ahikar looked at it and found another stone. He said, "My lord, I am a foreigner, and I have no tool for sewing. But I want you to command your faithful shoemakers to cut awls from this stone, that I may sew that millstone."

Then Pharaoh and all his nobles laughed. He said, "Blessed be the Highest God, who gave you this wit and knowledge."

When Pharaoh saw that Ahikar had overcome him, and answered his riddles, he at once became excited and commanded them to collect for him three years' tribute and to bring them to Ahikar. He stripped off his robes and put them on Ahikar, and his soldiers, and his servants, and gave him the expenses of his journey. He said to him, "Go in peace, strength of your lord and pride of your teachers. Does any king have one like you? Give my greetings to your lord King Sennacherib, and say to him how we have sent him gifts, for kings are content with little."

Then Ahikar arose, and kissed king Pharaoh's hands and kissed the ground in front of him, and wished him strength and continuance, and abundance in his treasury, and said to him, "My lord, I desire from you that not one of our countrymen may remain in Egypt."

Pharaoh rose and sent heralds to proclaim in the streets of Egypt that not one of the people of Nineveh in Assyria should remain in the land of Egypt, but that they should go with Ahikar. Then Ahikar left King Pharaoh and traveled to Nineveh in the land of Assyria and he had some treasures and a great deal of wealth. When the news reached King Sennacherib that Ahikar was coming, he went out to meet him and rejoiced over him exceedingly with great joy and embraced him and kissed him and said to him, "Welcome home, my relative, my brother Ahikar, the strength of my kingdom, and pride of my realm. Ask what you would have from me, even if you desire half of my kingdom and my possessions."

Then Ahikar said to him, "My lord king, live forever! Show favor, my lord king, to Abi Samik instead of me, for my life was in the hands of God and also his."

CHAPTER 6

Then King Sennacherib said, "Honor be to you, my beloved Ahikar! I will make the station of Abi Samik the swordsman, higher than all my trusted councilors and my favorites."

Then the king began to ask him how he had dealt with Pharaoh from when he arrived until he had left his presence, and how he had answered all his questions, and how he had received the tribute from him, and the changes of clothing and the presents. King Sennacherib celebrated with great joy, and said to Ahikar, "Take what you would have of this tribute, for it is all within your hands."

Ahikar replied, "Let the king live forever! I desire nothing but the safety of my lord king and the continuance of his greatness. My lord, what can I do with wealth and its like? But if you will show me favor, give me Nadan, my sister's son, that I may repay him for what he has done to me, and grant me his blood and hold me guiltless of it."

Sennacherib the king said, "Take him, I have given him to you."

Ahikar took Nadan, his sister's son, and bound his hands with chains of iron, and took him to his home, and put heavy shackles on his feet, and tied it with a tight knot, and after binding him so he threw him into a dark room, beside the retiring-place, and appointed Nebu-hal as watchman over him to give him a loaf of bread and a little water every day.

CHAPTER 6

CHAPTER 6 NOTES

1 Aramaic: prśḥå (אחזײ?). Translation: parasang (or league)

• Greek: parasángēs (παρασάγγης). Translation: parasang (or league)

• Armenian: hrasax (Հրասախ). Translation: parasang (or league)

• Arabic: farsak͟ (فَرْسَخ). Translation: parasang (or league)

The unit of measurement used in the text was the parasang, a Persian unit that was adopted by many other cultures. The term is accepted as having been adopted by other cultures during the Persian era, meaning it must have been a Persian era replacement for an older term. Its length was not consistent, ranging between 4.8 and 5.6 km (3 to 3½ miles). The term could not have been the original term in the text, as 68 parasangs would have only been about 340 km (200 miles), while the distance from the Egyptian capital of Sais to Nineveh would have been 1500 to 1600 kilometers (900 to 1000 miles), depending on the route taken.

The earlier Mesopotamian unit of measurement which is also translated into English as "league," was the bêr (𒁀𒀳), which was approximately 2.7 km (1.7 miles) long, even shorter than the parasang. The text implies that the original unit of measurement that the king of Egypt used, was very long as there were only 68 of them between Egypt and Assyria. The longest Egyptian unit of measurement that appears to have been used at the time was the îtrw (𓇋𓏏𓂋𓅱), which is translated into English as the 'River-Measure League,' as it was a nautical distance. It was approximately 10.5 km (6.5 miles) long, which would make the distance listed approximately 714 km (444 miles), which is only half the distance from Sais to Nineveh. As the unit of measurement was nautical, and the distance mentioned was approximately the distance from Sais to the Assyrian ports in Lebanon, it is plausible that the original text

CHAPTER 6

was referring to the Assyrian Empire, and not the city of Nineveh itself.

CHAPTER 7

Whenever Ahikar went in or out, he chastised Nadan, his sister's son, saying, "Nadan, my boy, I have done to you all that is good and kind and you have rewarded me for it, with what is ugly and bad and with murder. My son, it is said in the proverbs, 'He who does not listen with his ears, they will make listen with the scruff of his neck.'"

Nadan asked, "Why are you angry with me?"

Ahikar said to him, "Because I raised you, and taught you, and gave you honor and respect and made you great, and reared you with the best of breeding, and seated you in my place that you might be my heir in the world, and you treated me with killing and repaid me with my ruin. But the Lord knew that I was wronged, and he saved me from the trap which you had set for me, for the Lord heals the broken hearts and hinders the envious and the haughty.

My boy, you have been to me like the scorpion which when it strikes on brass, pierces it.

My boy, you are like the gazelle who was eating the roots of the madder, and it adds to me today, but tomorrow they will tan they hide in my roots.

My boy, you have been like he who saw his comrade naked in the winter, and he took cold water and poured it on him.

CHAPTER 7

My boy, you have been to me like a man who took a stone and threw it up to the sky to stone the Lord with it. The stone did not hit and did not reach high enough, but it became the cause of guilt and sin.

My boy, if you had honored me and respected me and had listened to my words you would have been my heir and would have reigned over my dominions.

My son, know that if the tail of the dog or the pig were ten cubits long it would not approach the worth of the horse's even if it were like silk.

My boy! I thought that you would have been my heir at my death, and you through your envy and your insolence desired to kill me. But the Lord delivered me from your cunning.

My son, you have been to me like a trap which was set up on the dunghill, and there came a sparrow and found the trap set up. The sparrow asked the trap, "Why are you here?"

The trap answered, "I am praying here to God."

The lark also asked it, "What is the piece of wood that you hold?"

The trap replied, "That is a young oak-tree on which I lean at the time of prayer."

The lark asked, "What is that thing in your mouth?"

The trap answered, "That is bread and meat which I carry for all the hungry and the poor who come near to me."

CHAPTER 7

The lark asked, "Now then, may I come forward and eat, as I am hungry?"

The trap answered him, "Come forward."

The lark approached so it might eat, but the trap sprang up and seized the lark by its neck. The lark answered and said to the trap, "If that is your bread for the hungry God will not accept your alms and your kind deeds. If that is your fasting and your prayers, God accepts from you neither your fast or your prayer, and God will not perfect what is good concerning you."

My boy, you have been to me like a lion who made friends with a donkey, and the donkey kept walking before the lion for a time, and one day the lion sprang on the donkey and ate it up.

My boy, you have been to me like a weevil in the wheat, for it does nothing good, but spoils the wheat and eats it.

My boy, you have been like a man who sowed ten measures of wheat, and when it was harvest time, he arose and reaped it, and separated it, and threshed it, and struggled over it to the utmost, and it turned out to be ten measures, and its master said to it, "You lazy thing, you have not grown and you have not shrunk."

My boy, you have been to me like the partridge that had been thrown into the net, and she could not save herself, but she called out to the partridges, that she might get them caught in the net with her.

CHAPTER 7

My son, you have been to me like the cold dog and it went into the potter's house to get warm. When it had gotten warm, it began to bark at them, and they chased it out and beat it, that it might not bite them.

My son, you have been to me like the pig who went into the hot bath with people of quality, and when it came out of the hot bath, it saw a muddy hole and it went down and wallowed in it.

My son, you have been to me like the goat which joined its comrades on their way to the sacrifice, and it was unable to save itself.

My boy, the dog which is not fed through its hunting becomes food for flies.

My son, the hand which does not labor and plow and is greedy and cunning will be cut away from its shoulder.

My son, the eye in which light is not seen, the ravens will pick at it and pluck it out.

My boy, you have been to me like a tree whose branches they were cutting, and it said to them, "If something of me were not in your hands, verily you would be unable to cut me."

My boy, you are like the cat to who they said, "Stop stealing until we make you a chain of gold and feed you with sugar and almonds."

She replied, "I am not forgetful of the craft of my father and my mother."

CHAPTER 7

My son, you have been like the serpent riding on a thorn-bush when he was among a river, and a wolf saw them and said, "Mischief on mischief, and let him who is more mischievous than they direct both of them."

The serpent said to the wolf, "The lambs and the goats and the sheep which you have eaten all your life, will you return them to their fathers and their parents or not?"

The wolf answered, "No."

The serpent said to him, "I think that after myself you are the worst of us."

My boy, I fed you with good food and you did not feed me with dry bread.

My boy, I gave you sugared water to drink and good syrup, and you did not give me water from the well to drink.

My boy, I taught you and raised you, and you dug a hiding-place for me and hid me.

My boy, I brought you up with the best upbringing and trained you like a tall cedar, and you have twisted and bent me.

My boy, it was my hope concerning you that you would build me a fortified castle, that I might be concealed from my enemies in it, and you did become to me like one buried in the depth of the earth, but the Lord took pity on me and delivered me from your cunning.

CHAPTER 7

My boy, I wished you well, and you did reward me with evil and hatefulness, and now I would fain tear from your eyes, and make you food for dogs, and cut out your tongue, and take off your head with the edge of the sword, and repay you for your abominable deeds."

When Nadan heard this speech from his uncle Ahikar, he said, "My uncle! Deal with me according to your knowledge, and forgive my sins, for who is there who has sinned like me, or who is there who forgives like you? Accept me, my uncle! Now I will serve in your house, and groom your horses and sweep up the dung of your livestock, and feed your sheep, for I am wicked and you are righteous. I the guilty and you the forgiving."

Ahikar answered him, "My boy, you are like the tree which was fruitless beside the water, and its master decided to cut it down, and it said to him, 'Move me to another place, and if I do not carry fruit, cut me down.'

Its master said to it, 'You've been beside the water and have not borne fruit, how will you carry fruit when you are in another place?'

My boy, the old age of the eagle is better than the youth of the crow.

My boy, they told the wolf, 'Keep away from the sheep in case their dust should harm you.' The wolf said, 'The dregs of the sheep's milk are good for my eyes.'

CHAPTER 7

My boy, they made the wolf go to a school so he might learn to read and they said to him, 'Say A, B...' He said, 'Lamb, goat...'

My boy, they set the donkey down at the table and he fell and began to roll himself in the dust and one said, "Let him roll himself, for it is his nature, he will not change."

My boy, the saying has been confirmed which goes, 'If you beget a boy, call him your son, and if you teach a boy, call him your slave.'

My boy, he who does good, will meet with good; and he who does evil will meet with evil, for the Lord repays a man according to the measure of his work.

My boy, what will I say more to you than these sayings? The Lord knows what is hidden, and is acquainted with the mysteries and the secrets. He will repay you and will judge, between me and you, and will repay you according to all your deserve."

When Nadan heard that speech from his uncle Ahikar, he swelled up immediately and became like a blown-out canteen. His limbs swelled and his legs and his feet and his side, and he was torn and his belly burst and his intestines were scattered, and he died. His end was destruction, and he went to the grave. For he who digs a pit for his brother will fall into it, and he who sets up traps will be caught in them.

This is what happened and what we found about the Words of Ahikar. Praise God forever. Amen, and peace.

CHAPTER 7

This chronicle is finished with the help of God, may he be praised!

Amen, Amen, Amen.

RESTORATION: CHAPTER 1

This is the story of Ahikar[1] the sage, vizier of King Ashur-banipal,[2] and of Ahikar's nephew Nadan.[3]

There was a vizier in the days of King Ashurbanipal, son of King Esarhaddon[4] of Nineveh in Assyria, a wise man named Ahikar. He had a great fortune and a great deal of property, and he was skillful, wise, a philosopher in knowledge, and opinionated in government. He had married sixty women and had built a mansion for each of them. Yet he had no child by any of these women who could be his heir. He was very sad on account of this, and one day he assembled the astrologers and the learned men and the wizards and explained to them his condition and the matter of his barrenness. They said to him, "Go, sacrifice to the gods and beg them, maybe they will provide you with a son."

He did as they told him and offered sacrifices to the idols, and prayed to them and begged them with requests. They did not answer him even one word. He went away sad and dejected, departing with a pain at his heart. He returned and implored the Highest God,[5] and believed, begging him with a burning in his heart, saying, "Highest God, creator of the skies and the earth, creator of all created things! I beg you to give me a son, that I may be consoled by him, and that he may be present in my home, and that he may close my eyes, and that he may bury me."

Then there came to him a voice saying, "As you have relied first of all on carved statues, and have offered sacrifices to them, for this reason, you will remain childless your whole life. But adopt Nadan your sister's son, and make him your child and teach him what you've learned and your good breeding, and at your death, he will bury you."

Thereafter he took Nadan his sister's son, who was still an infant. He handed him over to eight wet-nurses, that they might suckle him and raise him. They raised him with good food and gentle training and silk clothing, and purple and crimson, and he was seated on couches of silk. When Nadan grew big and walked, shooting up like a tall cedar, he taught him good manners and writing and science and philosophy.

After many days King Ashurbanipal looked at Ahikar and saw that he had grown very old, and he said to him, "My honored friend, the skillful, trustworthy, wise governor, my secretary, my vizier, my chancellor, and director. You have grown very old and weighted with years, and your departure from this world must be near. Tell me who will have a place in my service after you."

Ahikar said to him, "My lord, may you live forever! There is Nadan my sister's son, I have adopted him as my child. I have brought him up and taught him my wisdom and knowledge."

The king said to him, "Ahikar, bring him into my presence so I may see him, and if I find him suitable put him in your place, and you will go your way, to take a rest and to live the remainder of your life in sweet repose."

Then Ahikar went and presented Nadan his sister's son. He paid homage and wished him power and honor. He looked at him and admired him and rejoiced in him and said to Ahikar, "Is this your son, Ahikar? I pray that God may preserve him. As you have served me and my father Esarhaddon so may this boy of your serve me and fulfill my desires, needs, and business, so that I may honor him and make him powerful for your sake."

Ahikar paid obeisance to the king and said to him, "May you live forever, my lord king! I ask you that you may be patient with my boy Nadan and forgive his mistakes, so he may serve you as it is fitting."

Then the king swore to him that he would make him the greatest of his favorites, and the most powerful of his friends and that he should be with him in all honor and respect. He kissed his hands and bid him farewell. He took Nadan, his sister's son with him and seated him in a parlor and set about teaching him night and day until he had filled him with wisdom and knowledge more than with bread and water.

RESTORATION: CHAPTER 1 NOTES

1 Aramaic: Åḥyqr (ܝܩ^ܢ܂)
- Greek: Aẖiaẖaros (Αχιαχαρος)
- Armenian Xikar (Խիկար)

- Arabic: Hayqār (حَيْقَار)
- Old Slavonic: Akyrios (ᚼᚹᚣᛒᚺᚱᚨᛋ)

The variations of the name Ahikar transliterated into various translations of the book indicate that most copies were made from the Aramaic version of the book. The Codex Sinaiticus' Tobit, chapter 11 also includes a direct translation of the Aramaic name as Aḵikar (Αχικαρ), confirming that the Aramaic translation of Tobit used the same name for him.

2 Aramaic: Snḥryb (𐡔𐡍𐡇𐡓𐡉𐡁)

- Greek: Sanacharibos (Σαναχάριβος)
- Armenian: Sinak'erib (Uḥûwṗﬔﬨḥṗ)
- Arabic: Snḥāryb (سنحاريب)

King Sîn-ahhī-erība (𒀭𒌍𒋀𒌍𒆗) was the king of the Assyrian Empire between 705 and 681 BCE. While all surviving versions of the Words of Ahikar agree that it was Sennacherib, the actual successor to Esarhaddon was Ashurbanipal, indicating that the name of Ashurbanipal was redacted. The oldest copy of the book, an Aramaic copy that had been in use at the Israelite Temple of Elephantine used the name Bel where the later translations substituted "God" or "Lord," indicating that the Aramaic translation was created in the Neo-Babylonian Empire, explaining why Ashurbanipal's name was removed from the text. Ashurbanipal devastated Babylonia and Elam during the civil/international war against his brother Shamash-shum-ukin and his allies in Elam in the 640s BCE. The Assyrians won the war, but at such a tremendous financial cost, and with such a loss of prestige, that Nabopolassar was able to lead another Babylonian revolt in the 620s BCE, a few years after Ashurbanipal's death. This rebellion drew in virtually all of Assyria's neighbors, and ultimately destroyed the Neo-Assyrian Empire, dividing its territory between the newly independent

Neo-Babylonian Empire, the Median Empire, and the Lydian Empire. When the Aramaic version of Ahikar was translated, Ashurbanipal would have been seen in a similar light to how Hitler was viewed after the Second World War, making his redaction from the text a necessity.

Additionally, Ahikar could not have worked for Sennacherib, who was one of the Assyrian Kings that conquered his homeland of Samaria and exiled his people. Sennacherib would not have sent a Samaritan captive to represent him in negotiations in Egypt or Elam. The Book of Tobit recorded that both Tobit and Ahikar worked for Esarhaddon, however, Ahikar was Tobit's nephew, and therefore would have continued to work for Esarhaddon's successor Ashurbanipal. Unfortunately, all known copies of Ahikar are based on the Aramaic translation, and therefore include this anachronism.

3 Aramaic: Ndn (𐤍𐤃𐤍)
- Greek: Nadab (Ναβαδ)
- Armenian: Nadin (Նադխū)
- Arabic: Nbāb (نباب)

Nadan's name is not standardized, and appears to have diverged during the Persian era. This translation uses the Aramaic variant of Ndn, which is probably the original, and certainly served as the source for the Armenian variant of Nadin. The Greek of Nabab and Arabic variant of Nbāb, probably reflect a Persian era Moabite reinterpretation within the Aramaic versions of Ahikar. Ndb (𐤍𐤃𐤁) was a Moabite word meaning "willing," and often used in religious context for one who is 'willing to serve a god,' such as the name Kmš-ndb (𐤊𐤌𐤔𐤍𐤃𐤁), a Moabite king who agreed to pay tribute to Assyria after Sennacherib's Levantine Wars.

4 Aramaic: Åsrḥdwn (אסרחדון)

• Greek: Esarhaddon (Εσαρχαδδών)

• Arabic: Åsrḥdwn (آسرحدون)

Aššur-aḫa-iddina, more commonly known as Esarhaddon from the Hebrew version of his name 'Ēsar-ḥaddōn (אֵסַר־חַדֹּן) was actually Sennacherib's son, not his father. Esarhaddon was the king of the Assyrian Empire between 681 and 669 BCE. He is famous for conquering Egypt and creating the largest Empire in Middle-eastern history until then.

5 The Highest is a reference to God, or a god, found in many ancient religions in the region. According to the Torah, the ancient people of Jerusalem worshiped 'ēl 'elyôn (אֵל עֶלְיוֹן), which translates as 'God highest' when Abraham passed through the region. The Greeks translated it as Ṭeō tō usistō (Θεω τω υψιστω) in the Septuagint, also meaning 'God the highest.' El elyon is known to have been a major god of the Canaanites, called âl wâlyn (𐤀𐤋 𐤅𐤀𐤋𐤉𐤍), meaning 'God and highest' in an Aramaic language Sefire Treaty from circa 750 BCE. The Greek translations of Sanchuniathon's bronze age writing that have survived to the present, referred to the primordial creator god of the Canaanites as Elioun (Ελιουν), which appears to be the same god. According to Sanchuniathon, Elioun was the "highest" (υψιστος) god, who made the sky and the land, and they made the rest of the gods. While the many references to Bel in this text appear to refer to the Babylonian god Bel, these references to the Highest are clearly references to the old Canaanite god El elyon. A version of El elyon was worshiped by the Neo-Assyrians in the form of deityŠar (𒀭𒊬), more commonly called Anshar today. Anshar translates directly as 'deity totality' or 'deity eternity,' and was perceived in the later Neo-Assyrian era as the patriarch of the gods who created everything.

Restoration: Chapter 2

He taught him, saying, "My son! Hear my speech and follow my advice and remember what I say.

My son, if you hear a word, let it remain in your heart, and don't reveal it to another, in case it becomes a lump of burning coal and burns your tongue and causes pain in your body, and you become reproachful and are shamed before God and man.

My son, if you have heard a report, don't spread it, and if you have seen something, don't tell it.

My son, make your speech easy to the listener and do not rush to answer questions.

My son, when you have heard anything, don't hide it.

My son, don't loosen a sealed knot, or untie it, and don't seal a loosened knot.

My son, don't covet outward beauty, for it fades and passes away, but instead an honorable memory that lasts forever.

My son, don't let a foolish woman deceive you with her speech, in case you die the most miserable of deaths, and she entangles you in a net until you are trapped.

My son, don't desire a woman beautified with clothing and with ointments, who is despicable and foolish in her mind. Woe to you if you bestow on her anything that is yours or commit to her what is in your hand and she entices you into sin, and God becomes angry with you.

My son, do not be like the almond-tree, for it brings out leaves before all the trees, and edible fruit after them all, but be like the mulberry-tree, which brings out edible fruit before all the trees, and leaves after them all.

My son, bend your head low down, and soften your voice, and be courteous, and walk in the straight path, and don't be foolish. Don't raise your voice when you laugh for if it were by a loud voice that a house was built, the donkey would build many houses every day, and if it were just through strength that the plow was driven, the plow would never be removed from under the shoulders of the camels.

My son, the moving of stones with a wise man is better than the drinking of wine with a foolish man.

My son, pour out your wine on the tombs of the just and don't drink with ignorant, contemptible people.

My son, cling to wise men who fear God and be like them, and don't go near the ignorant, in case you become like him and learn his ways.

My son, when you have a comrade or a friend, test him, and afterward make him a comrade and a friend, and do not praise him without testing him. Do not waste your speech with a man who lacks wisdom.

My son, while a shoe stays on your foot, walk with it on the thorns, and make a road for your son, and for your household and your children, and make your ship taut before she goes on the sea and its waves and sinks and cannot be saved.

My son, if the rich man eats a snake, they say, "It is through his wisdom," and if a poor man eats it, the people say, "Because he is hungry."

My son, be content with your daily bread and your goods and don't covet what is another's.

My son, don't be neighbor to the fool, and don't eat bread with him, and don't rejoice in the calamities of your neighbors. If your enemy wrongs you, show him kindness.

My son, a man who fears God, fears him and honors him.

My son, the ignorant man falls and stumbles, and the wise man, even if he stumbles is not shaken, and even if he falls, he gets up quickly, and if he is sick he can take care of his life. But as for the ignorant, stupid man, there is no drug for his disease.

My son, if a man approaches you who is inferior to yourself, go forward to meet him and remain on your feet. If he cannot repay you, his lord will repay you for him.

My son, don't spare beating your son, for the beating of your son is like manure to the garden, and like tying the opening of a purse, and like the tethering of beasts, and like the bolting of the door.

My son, restrain your son from wickedness, and teach him manners before he rebels against you and brings you into contempt among the people and you hang your head in the streets and the assemblies and you be punished for the evil of his wicked deeds.

My son, get a fat ox with a foreskin, and a donkey with great hoofs, and don't get an ox with large horns, or make friends with a deceitful man, or get a quarrelsome slave, or a thievish handmaid, for everything which you give to them they will ruin.

My son, don't let your parents curse you, and the Lord[1] be pleased with them, for it has been said, "He who despises his father or his mother, let him die the death and he who honors his parents will prolong his days and his life and will see all that is good."

My son, don't travel the road without weapons, for you don't know when a foe may meet you, and you should be ready for him.

My son, do not be like a bare, leafless tree that does not grow, but be like a tree covered with its leaves and its boughs, for the man who has neither wife nor children is disgraced in the world and is hated by them, like a leafless and fruitless tree.

My son, be like a fruitful tree on the roadside, whose fruit is eaten by all who pass by, and the beasts of the desert rest under its shade and eat of its leaves.

My son, every sheep that wanders from its path and its companions becomes food for the wolf.

My son, don't say, "My lord is a fool and I am wise," and don't relate the speech of ignorance and folly, in case you become hated by him.

My son, don't be one of those servants, to who their lords say, "Get away from us," but be one of those to whom they say, "Approach and come near to us."

My son, don't caress your slave in the presence of his companion, for you don't know which of them will be of most value to you in the end.

My son, don't be afraid of the Lord who created you, in case he is silent to you.

My son, make your speech fair and sweeten your tongue, and don't let your companion step on your foot, in case at another time he steps on your chest.

My son, if you defeat a wise man with a word of wisdom, it will lurk in his chest like a subtle sense of shame, but if you beat the ignorant with a stick he will neither understand nor hear.

My son, if you send a wise man for your needs, do not give him many orders, for he will do your business as you desire, and if you send a fool, do not order him, but go yourself and do your business, for if you order him, he will not do what you desire. If they send you on business, hurry to fulfill it quickly.

My son, don't make an enemy of a man stronger than yourself, for he will take your measure, and his revenge on you.

My son, test your son, and your servant, before you trust your belongings to them, in case they run away with them, for he who has a full hand is called wise, even if he is stupid and ignorant, and he who has an empty hand is called poor and ignorant, even if he is the prince of sages.

My son, I have eaten colocynth,[2] and swallowed bitters, and I have found nothing more bitter than poverty and scarcity.

My son, teach your son frugality and hunger, that he may do well in the management of his household.

My son, don't teach the ignorant the language of wise men, for it will be burdensome to him.

My son, don't display your condition to your friend, in case you become despised by him.

My son, the blindness of the heart is more terrible than the blindness of the eyes, for the blindness of the eyes may be guided little by little, but the blindness of the heart is not guided, and it leaves the straight path and goes in a crooked way.

My son, the stumbling of a man with his foot is better than the stumbling of a man with his tongue.

My son, a friend who is near is better than a more excellent brother who is far away.

82

RESTORATION: CHAPTER 2

My son, beauty fades but learning lasts, and the world fades and becomes vain, but a good name neither becomes vain nor fades.

My son, for the man who has no peace, his death is better than his life, and the sound of mourning is better than the sound of singing. If the fear of God is in them, sorrow and weeping are better than the sound of singing and rejoicing.

My child, the leg of a frog in your hand is better than a goose in the pot of your neighbor, and a sheep near you is better than an ox far away, and a sparrow in your hand is better than a thousand sparrows flying. Poverty which gathers is better than the scattering of many provisions, and a living fox is better than a dead lion. A pound of wool is better than a pound of gold or silver, for the gold and the silver are hidden and covered up in the earth and are not seen, but the wool stays in the markets and it is seen, and it is a beauty to him who wears it.

My son, a small fortune is better than a scattered fortune.

My son, a living dog is better than a dead poor man.

My son, a poor man who does right is better than a rich man who is dead because of his sins.

My son, keep a word in your heart, and it will be much to you and beware that you don't reveal the secret of your friend.

My son, don't let a word issue from your mouth until you have taken counsel with your heart. Stand not between quarreling people, because from an insult there comes a quarrel, and from a quarrel there comes a dispute, and from dispute there comes fighting, and you will be forced to bear witness. Instead, run from there and have peace.

My son, don't struggle with a man stronger than yourself, but have a patient spirit, and endure in upright conduct, for there is nothing more excellent than that.

My son, don't hate your first friend, for the second one may not last.

My son, visit the poor in his affliction, and speak of him in the king's presence, and do your diligence to save him from the mouth of the lion.

My son, don't rejoice in the death of your enemy, for after a little while you will be his neighbor, and he who mocks you, you respect and honor and greeting him first.

My son, if water would stand still in the sky, and a black crow become white, and myrrh grows sweet as honey, then ignorant men and fools might understand and become wise.

My son, if you desire to be wise, restrain your tongue from lying, and your hand from stealing, and your eyes from seeing evil, and then you will be called wise.

My son, let the wise man beat you with a wand but don't let the fool anoint you with sweet salve. Be humble in your youth and you will be honored in your old age.

My son, don't stand against a man in the days of his power, or a river in the days of its flood.

My son, do not rush to wed a wife, for if it turns out well, she will say, "My lord, make provision for me," and if it turns out poorly, she will accuse him who was the cause of it.

My son, whoever is elegant in his dress, he is the same in his speech, and he who has a mean appearance in his dress, he also is the same in his speech.

My son, if you have committed a theft, make it known to the king, and give him a share of it, that you may be delivered from him, for otherwise, you will endure bitterness.

My son, make a friend of the man whose hand is satisfied and filled and don't make friends with the man whose hand is closed and hungry.

There are four things in which neither the king nor his army can be secure: oppression by the vizier, bad government, perversion of the will, and tyranny over the subjects, and four things which cannot be hidden: the prudent, the foolish, the rich, and the poor."

Restoration: Chapter 2 Notes

1 Aramaic: Bôlâ (ℵℓⵁⴄ). Translation: Bel (or Ba'al, Lord)
- Greek: Kurios (Κύριος). Translation: lord
- Armenian: Ter (Stn). Translation: owner (or lord, master)
- Arabic: āllh (الله). Translation: god
- Old Slavonic: Gospodĭ (ⰃⰑⰔⰒⰑⰄⰠ). Translation: lord (or master)

The various later translations indicate that the Christian and/or Islamic God is being referred to, however, scholars believe the Aramaic version was referring to Bel, the supreme god of the Neo-Babylonian pantheon. If this analysis is correct, it means the Neo-Assyrian Cuneiform text of Ahikar must have been translated into Aramaic in the Neo-Babylonian Empire, which supports the removal of the name of Ashurbanipal. Bel was worshiped by the Babylonians in the first millennium BCE. He was a syncretization of the older Mesopotamian Marduk, Enlil, and Dumuzid. However, his name simply translates as "Lord," meaning that Ahikar could have simply been using the term "Lord."

Whichever god Ahikar was referring to, if he was living in Assyria under Ashurbanipal, he would not have been worshiping the god of the renegade Neo-Babylonians, meaning that Bel can only be accepted as the original god in the text if it is assumed that Ahikar did not exist, and the book is a work of fiction, written in the Neo-Babylonian era. However, this also seems improbable, as a book about a Samaritan worshiper of Bel living in the Neo-Assyrian Empire, should anyone decide to write something so obscure, would have been written in Neo-Babylonian Cuneiform, and probably not translated into Aramaic until the Persian era, resulting in the reading of 'Bel' being erased by the Israelites abandoning the title Ba'al for their god during the Neo-Babylonian era in response Bel being the supreme god of the people who destroyed Jerusalem. As the setting of the book is Assyria, not Babylonia, the Assyrian reading of Belu (-𒂗) is used in this translation, generally rendering the term as 'Lord,' as it appears in Greek, Aramaic, and Old Slavonic translations.

There are specific references to an Idol of Bel / Lord / Allah, however, as there was no known statue at the time of the Lord or Allah, the translation of Bel is used, however, it is unlikely Bel was originally in the Neo-Assyrian text. The references to the Idol of

Bel, take place in "Egypt," which may have been Kush at the time when Ahikar was speaking to the Pharaoh, indicating that the author was referring to an Egyptian or Kushite god, not a Babylonian god. As the name of the god is no longer in any of the texts, the reference to Bel is used in relation to the idol.

2 Colocynth, also called bitter apples, is a vine native to the Mediterranean region and was once cultivated across Anatolia, the Middle East, Egypt, and Kush. It was cultivated in Egypt since pre-Dynastic times, since at least 3800 BCE. By the classical era, it was mainly used for medicine. Today it is primarily cultivated for medicine or bio-fuel.

RESTORATION: CHAPTER 3

So spoke Ahikar, and when he had finished these injunctions and proverbs to Nadan, his sister's son, he imagined that he would keep them all, and he did not know that instead, that he was seeing him as weary and contemptible, and mocking him. Ahikar sat in his house afterward and gave to Nadan all his goods, and the slaves, and the handmaidens, and the horses, and the livestock, and everything else that he had possessed and gained, and the power of bidding and of forbidding was given to the hand of Nadan. Ahikar sat in peace in his house, and occasionally Ahikar went and paid his respects to the king, and returned home.

When Nadan saw that the power of bidding and forbidding was in his hands, he despised the position of Ahikar and scoffed at him, and set about blaming him whenever he appeared, saying, "My uncle Ahikar is in his old age, and he knows nothing anymore."

He began to beat the slaves and the handmaidens and to sell the horses and the camels and he spent all that his uncle Ahikar had owned. When Ahikar saw that he had no compassion on his servants or his household, he arose and chased him from his house, and sent a message to inform the king that he had scattered his possessions and his provision.

The king arose and called Nadan and said to him, "While Ahikar remains in health, no one will rule his goods, or his household, or over his possessions."

The hand of Nadan was lifted off from his uncle Ahikar and all his goods, and in the meantime, he neither went in or out nor did he greet him. Afterward, Ahikar regretted the struggle with Nadan his sister's son, and he continued to be very sad. Nadan had a younger brother named Benuzardan, so Ahikar took him for himself instead of Nadan, and raised him and honored him with the greatest honors. He gave over to him all that he possessed and made him ruler of his house.

Now when Nadan found out what had happened he was seized with envy and jealousy, and he began to complain to everyone who questioned him, and to mock his, uncle Ahikar, saying, "My uncle has chased me from his house and has preferred my brother to me, but if the Highest God gives me the power, I will cause him to be killed."

Nadan thought about what trap he might set for him. After a while, Nadan turned it over in his mind and wrote a letter to Bel-Iqisha,[1] servant of King Teumman,[2] the king of Elam,[3] saying:

> *"Peace and health and strength and honor from Ashurbanipal, king of Nineveh in Assyria, and from his vizier and his secretary Ahikar to you, great king! Let there be peace between you and me.*
>
> *When this letter reaches you, if you will rise and go quickly to the plains of the protectors,[4] and to Nineveh*

*in Assyria, I will deliver up the kingdom to you with-
out war and without a battle-formation."*

He wrote also another letter in the name of Ahikar to
Pharaoh king of Egypt:[5]

*"Let there be peace between you and me, mighty
king!*

*If at the time when this letter reaches you, you rise
and go to Nineveh in Assyria to the plain of the protectors, I will deliver up to you the kingdom without war
and without fighting."*

The letters of Nadan looked like the letters of his uncle
Ahikar. He folded the two letters and sealed them with the
seal of his uncle Ahikar, and they were left in the king's
palace. Then he went and wrote a similar letter from the king
to his uncle Ahikar:

*"Peace and health to my vizier, my secretary, my
chancellor, Ahikar,*

*Ahikar, when this letter reaches you, assemble all
the soldiers who are with you, and let them be in perfect clothing and in great numbers, and bring them to
me on the fifth day in the plain of the protectors.*

*When you see me there coming towards you,
quickly have the army move against me like an enemy
who would fight with me, for I have with me the ambassadors of Pharaoh king of Egypt, that they may see
the strength of our army and may fear us, for they are*

our enemies and they hate us."

Then he sealed the letter and sent it to Ahikar by one of the king's servants. He took the other letter which he had written and spread it before the king and read it to him and showed him the seal. When the king heard what was in the letter he was perplexed and greatly confused and fiercely angry, and said, "Oh, I have been shown wisdom! What have I done to Ahikar that he has written these letters to my enemies? Is this my repayment for my gifts to him?"

Nadan said to him, "Do not be sad, king! Nor be angry, but let us go to the plain of the protectors and see if the story is true or not."

Then Nadan arose on the fifth day and took the king and the soldiers and the vizier, and they went to the desert to the plain of the protectors. The king looked and saw Ahikar and the army set in formation. When Ahikar saw that the king was there, he approached and signaled to the army to move as they would in war and to fight in formation against the king as it had been told in the letter, not knowing the trap Nadan had set for him.

When the king saw the acts of Ahikar he was seized with anxiety and terror and confusion and was very angry. Nadan said to him, "Have you seen, my lord the king, what this wretch has done? Do not be angry and do not be sad or hurt, but go to your house and sit on your throne, and I will bring Ahikar to you bound and chained with chains, and I will chase away your enemy from before you without a battle."

The king returned to his throne, being provoked about Ahikar, and did nothing about him. Nadan went to Ahikar and said to him, "Hello, my uncle! The king is very happy with you, and thanks you for having done what he commanded you. Now he has sent me to you that you may dismiss the soldiers to their duties and come yourself to him with your hands bound behind you, and your feet chained, that the ambassadors of Pharaoh may see this and that the king may be feared by them and by their king."

Then Ahikar answered, "To hear is to obey."

He arose right away and bound his hands behind him, and chained his feet, and Nadan took him to the king. When Ahikar entered the king's presence he did obeisance before him on the ground and wished for power and perpetual life to the king. Then the king demanded, "Ahikar, my secretary, the governor of my affairs, my chancellor, the ruler of my state, tell me what evil have I done to you that you have rewarded me by this terrible deed."

Then they showed him the letters in his writing and with his seal. When Ahikar saw this, his limbs trembled and his tongue was tied at once, and he was unable to speak a word from fear, but he hung his head towards the earth and was dumb. When the king saw this, he felt certain that the scheme was from him, and he immediately rose and commanded them to execute Ahikar and to chop his neck with the sword outside of the city. Then Nadan screamed and said, "Ahikar! What makes you thing you can do things to the king?"

(So says the story-teller.)

The name of the swordsman was Abi Samik. The king said to him, "Swordsman! Rise and go cut the neck of Ahikar at the door of his house, and throw away his head from his body a hundred cubits."

Then Ahikar knelt before the king, and said, "Let my lord the king live forever! If you desire to slay me, let your wish be fulfilled, and I know that I am not guilty, but the wicked man has to give an account of his wickedness, nevertheless, my lord the king, I beg of you and from your friendship, permit the swordsman to give my body to my slaves, that they may bury me, and let your slave be your sacrifice."

The king rose and commanded the swordsman to do with him according to his desire. He immediately commanded his servants to take Ahikar and the swordsman and take him naked, so they might slay him. When Ahikar knew for certain that he was to be slain he sent a message to his wife, and said to her, "Come out and meet me, and let there be with you a thousand young virgins, and dress them in gowns of purple and silk that they may cry for me before my death. Prepare a table for the swordsman and his servants, and prepare plenty of wine, that they may drink."

She did all that he commanded her. She was very wise, clever, and prudent. She united all possible courtesy and learning. When the army of the king and the swordsman arrived, he found the table set in order, and the wine and the luxurious viands, and they began eating and drinking till they were gorged and drunken.

Then Ahikar took the swordsman aside, separate from the company and said, "Abi Samik, do you not know that when Esarhaddon the king, the father of Ashurbanipal, wanted to kill you, I took you and hid you in a certain place until the king's anger subsided and he asked for you?"

"When I brought you into his presence he rejoiced in you, and now remember the kindness I did you. I know that the king will be sorry about me and will be very angry about my execution. For I am not guilty, and it will happen when you present me before him in his palace, you will meet with great fortune, and know that Nadan my sister's son has deceived me and has done this terrible deed to me, and the king will repent of having killed me. I have a well in the garden of my house, and no one knows of it. Hide me in it with only my wife knowing. I have a slave in prison who deserves to be killed. Bring him out and dress him in my clothes, and command the servants when they are drunk to slay him. They will not know who it is they are killing. Throw away his head a hundred cubits from his body, and give his body to my slaves that they may bury it. You have laid up a great treasure with me."

Then the swordsman did as Ahikar had commanded him, and he went to the king and said to him, "May you live forever!"

Then each week, Ahikar's wife lowered down to him in his hiding-place everything he needed, and no one else knew of it. The story was reported and repeated and spread abroad in every place of how Ahikar the Sage had been slain and was dead, and all the people of that city mourned for him. They wept and said, "Alas for you, Ahikar, and for your learning and your courtesy! How sad it is to lose you and your knowledge! Where can another like you be found? Where can there be a man so intelligent, learned, and skilled in ruling as to resemble you that he may fill your place?"

The king repented killing Ahikar, but his repentance did not help him. Then he called for Nadan and said to him, "Go, and take your friends with you, and mourn and cry for your uncle Ahikar, and lament for him as is the custom, honoring in his memory."

But when Nadan, the foolish, the ignorant, the hardhearted, went to the house of his uncle, he neither wept nor mourned nor wailed, but assembled heartless and dissolute people and set about eating and drinking. Nadan began to seize the woman-slaves and the men-slaves belonging to Ahikar, and bound them and tortured them and beat them severely. He did not respect the wife of his uncle, she who had brought him up like her own son, but wanted her to sin with him. Ahikar had been in the hiding-place, and he heard the weeping of his slaves and his neighbors, and he praised the Highest God, the Merciful One, and gave thanks, and he continued to pray and implore the Highest God.

The swordsman came from time to time to Ahikar while he was in the hiding-place, and Ahikar came and begged him. He comforted him and wished him deliverance. When the story was reported in other countries that Ahikar the Sage had been murdered, all the kings were sad and hated king Ashurbanipal, and they lamented over Ahikar the solver of riddles.

RESTORATION: CHAPTER 3 NOTES

1 Aramaic: Åkẏš (𐡀𐡊𐡉𐡔)

- Greek: Akǩous (Ακχους)
- Armenian: Akhis (Ախիս)
- Arabic: Åẖyš (أخيش)

While the text refers to this as the son of "King Wise of Persia," it is likely that this began as a reference the Aramean chieftain Bel-Iqisha, who led an Elamite backed rebellion in southern Babylonian in 665 BCE. Åkẏš (𐤀𐤊𐤉𐤔) was also a popular Canaanite name at the time, and several Philistine kings bore the name, which was recorded in Neo-Assyrian Cuneiform as Ikaúsu (𒄿𒅗𒌑𒋢).

2 All translations refer to a 'King Wise, however, there are no records of any Persian king named any variation of the word 'wise,' and at Persia did not exist as a kingdom at the time, this was probably a mistranslation of the name of the Elamite king Teumman, who backed the rebellion of Bel-Iqisha in 664 BCE. Teumman's name was virtually the same as the Babylonian word tēmānu (𒈨𒉪), which meant "wise," suggesting that the original

Neo-Assyrian story was about King Teumman and his proxy Bel-Iqisha.

3 All translations that survive to the present refer to this land as Persia, however, the Book of Tobit refers to it as Elam. This suggests that the term Persia was used in the original Aramaic translation made in the Neo-Babylonian Empire, which appears to have served for all later translations. This is historically valid, as Persia became a kingdom during the Neo-Babylonian era, and Elam no longer existed by the time that Babylon and its allies overthrew Assyria.

4 The word Nisrin, appear to be a Persian reinterpretation of the older Neo-Assyrian cuneiform word naṣārum (𒈾𒊕𒌝). The Persian word nasrin (نسرین) means roses, while the Akkadian word meant 'protectors.' As the described geography places the Plain of Roses/Protectors in the region around Nineveh, and the Assyrians spoke Assyrian, and not Persian, the original meaning is restored.

5 All translations agree that this was Egypt, which if the previous references were to Bel-Iqisha and King Teumman in 664 BCE, would make this the first regal year of Pharaoh Wahibre Psamtik I, however, at the beginning of his reign he did not control Egypt, as the Kushites had invaded and captured most of the country, and in the process killed his predecessor Pharaoh Necho I. If Nadan had sent a letter to the king of Egypt at the time it would have been King Tantamani of Kush, who was at war against Assyria. The following year, 663 BCE, the Assyrian army reinvaded Egypt and drove out the Kushites, and spent the next few years occupying southern Egypt, meaning it could not have been later than 664 BCE.

Restoration: Chapter 4

When the king of Egypt[1] had heard that Ahikar was dead, he rose immediately and wrote a letter to King Ashurbanipal, saying:

"Peace, health, might, and honor which we wish especially for you, my beloved brother, king Ashurbanipal.

I have been desiring to build a castle in the air between the sky and the earth, and I want you to send me a wise, clever man from yourself to build it for me, and to answer me all my questions, and that I may have the tribute and the custom duties of Assyria for three years."

Then he sealed the letter and sent it to Ashurbanipal, who took it and read it and gave it to his viziers and to the nobles of his kingdom, and they were confused and ashamed. He was very angry and was puzzled about how he should act. Then he assembled the old men and the learned men and the wise men and the philosophers, and the diviners and the astrologers, and everyone who was in his country, and read them the letter and said to them, "Who among you will go to Pharaoh king of Egypt and answer his riddles?"

They answered him, "Our lord king, you know that there is none in your kingdom who is acquainted with these riddles except Ahikar, your vizier and secretary. But as for us, we have no skill in this, unless it is Nadan, his sister's son, for he taught him all his wisdom and learning and knowledge. Call him to you, maybe he may untie this difficult knot."

Then the king called Nadan and said to him, "Look at this letter and understand what is in it."

When Nadan read it, he said, "My lord, who is able to build a castle in the air between the sky and the earth?"

When the king heard the question of Nadan he was very sad, and climbed down from his throne and sat in the ashes, and began to cry and wail over Ahikar saying, "My grief! Ahikar, who knew the secrets and the riddles! Woe to me, Ahikar! Teacher of my country and ruler of my kingdom, where will I find another like you? Ahikar, teacher of my country, where will I turn for you? Woe to me over you! How could I destroy you, and I listened to the talk of a stupid, ignorant boy without knowledge, without religion, without manliness. Why, and why again? Who can give you to me just for once, or bring me word that Ahikar is alive? I would give him half of my kingdom! What is this to me? Oh, Ahikar! That I might see you just once more. Oh! My grief for you, for all time! Ahikar, why have I killed you, and did not delay your case until I had seen all the information?"

The king went on weeping night and day, and when the swordsman saw the anger of the king and his sorrow for Ahikar, his heart was softened towards him, and he entered into his presence and said to him, "My lord! Command your servants to cut off my head."

Then the king asked him, "Why Abi Samik, what is your fault?"

The swordsman said to him, "My master! Every slave who acts contrary to the word of his master is killed, and I have acted contrary to your command."

Then the king asked him, "Why Abi Samik? In what way have you disobeyed my command?"

The swordsman answered him, "My lord! You commanded me to kill Ahikar, and I knew that you would have regret concerning him and that he had been wronged, and I hid him in a certain place, and I killed one of his slaves, and he is now safe in the well, and if you command me I will bring him to you."

The king said to him, "Shame on you, Abi Samik! You are mocking me and I am your lord."

The swordsman replied to him, "No, but by your life, my lord! Ahikar is safe and alive."

When the king heard this, he felt sure of the matter, and his head swam, and he fainted from joy. He commanded them to bring Ahikar. He said to the swordsman, "Trusty servant! If your words are true, I will greatly enrich you, and praise you above all your friends."

The swordsman went out rejoicing and traveled to Ahikar's house. He opened the door of the hiding-place, and went down and found Ahikar sitting, praising God, and thanking him. He called to him, saying, "Ahikar, I bring the greatest of joy, and happiness, and delight!"

Ahikar asked him, "What is the news, Abi Samik?"

He told him all about Pharaoh from the beginning to the end. Then he took him and went to the king. When the king looked at him, he saw him in a state of need, and that his hair had grown long like the wild beasts' and his nails were like the claws of an eagle, and that his body was dirty with dust, and the color of his face had changed and faded and was now like ashes. When the king saw him he was sad because of him and rose at once and embraced him and kissed him, and wept over him and said, "Praise the god who has brought you back to me."

Then he consoled him and comforted him. He stripped off his robe, and put it on the swordsman, and was very gracious to him, and gave him great wealth, and gave Ahikar peace. Then Ahikar said to the king, "Let my lord the king live forever! These are the deeds of the children of the world. I have raised a palm-tree that I might lean on it, and it bent sideways and threw me down. My lord, since I have appeared before you, don't let concerns oppress you!"

The king said to him, "Blessed is the god, who showed you mercy, and knew that you were wronged, and saved you and delivered you from being slain. Go to the warm bath, and shave your head, and cut your nails, and change your clothes, and amuse yourself for forty days, that you may be good to yourself and improve your condition and the color of your face may come back to you."

Then the king stripped off his costly robe and put it on Ahikar, and Ahikar thanked God and did obeisance to the king, and departed to his house glad and happy, praising the Highest God. The people of his household rejoiced with him, and his friends and everyone who heard that he was alive rejoiced also.

RESTORATION: CHAPTER 4 NOTES

1 Assuming that the original Assyrian king in the story was Ashurbanipal, then this would have to be King Psamtik I, who ruled Egypt from 663 BCE, when Ashurbanipal placed him on the throne of Egypt as an Assyrian vassal to 610 BCE, several decades after the fall of Assyria. There are no surviving records of him attempting to build a castle in the sky, or anything else of significance. Most of his reign seems to have been focused on military campaigns and politics. He managed to defend Egypt from any further Kushite incursions, and successfully transitioned the country from being an Assyrian vassal to an independent nation. After Assyria fell, he spent the next few couple of decades competing with the Babylonians for control of Canaan.

RESTORATION: CHAPTER 5

He did as the king commanded him, and rested for forty days. Then he dressed himself in his nicest clothes, and rode to the king, with his slaves behind him and before him, rejoicing and delighted. But when Nadan saw what was happening, fear took hold of him and terror, and he was confused, not knowing what to do. When Ahikar saw it he entered into the king's presence and greeted him, and he returned the greeting, and made him sit down at his side, saying to him, "My friend Ahikar! Look at these letters which the king of Egypt sent to us after he heard that you were killed. They have provoked us and confused us, and many of the people of our country have fled to Egypt in fear of the tribute that the king of Egypt has demanded from us."

Then Ahikar took the letter and read it, and understood its contents. Then he said to the king, "Do not be angry, my lord! I will go to Egypt, and I will return the answers to Pharaoh, and I will display this letter to him, and I will reply to him about the tribute, and I will send back all those who have run away, and I will put your enemies to shame with the help of the Highest God, and for the happiness of your kingdom."

When the king heard this speech from Ahikar he rejoiced greatly, and his heart was expanded and he showed him favor. Ahikar asked the king, "Grant me a delay of forty days that I may consider this question and answer it."

The king permitted this, and Ahikar returned to his home. He commanded the hunters to capture two young eagles for him, and they captured them and brought them to him. He commanded the weavers of ropes to weave two cotton ropes for him, each two thousand cubits long. He had the carpenters brought to him and ordered them to make two great boxes, which they did. Then he took two young boys, and spent every day sacrificing lambs, and feeding the eagles and the boys. He made the boys ride on the backs of the eagles, and he bound them with a firm knot, and tied the cable to the feet of the eagles, and let them soar upwards little by little every day, to a distance of ten cubits, until they grew used to it and were trained to do it. They rose all the length of the rope until they reached the sky, with the boys on their backs. Then he pulled them back to himself.

When Ahikar saw that his plan was working he ordered the boys that when they were carried up into the sky, they were to shout, "Bring us clay and stone, so we can build a castle for king Pharaoh, as we are idle."

Ahikar was never done training them and exercising them until they had reached the highest possible place. Then leaving them he went to the king and said to him, "My lord! The work is finished as to your desire. Rise with me that I may show you the wonder."

So the king got up and sat with Ahikar and went to a wide place and sent to bring the eagles and the boys, and Ahikar tied them and let them up into the air all the length of the ropes, and they began to shout as he had taught them. Then he drew them to himself and put them in their places. The king and those who were with him wondered greatly, and the king kissed Ahikar between his eyes and said to him, "Go in peace, my friend, pride of my kingdom, to Egypt and answer the riddles of Pharaoh and overcome him by the strength of the Highest God."

Then he commanded him farewell, and took his troops and his army and the young men and the eagles, and went towards the dwellings of Egypt, and when he had arrived, he turned towards the country of the king.

When the people of Egypt knew that Ashurbanipal had sent a man of his trusted council to talk with Pharaoh and to answer his questions, they took the news to king Pharaoh, and he sent a party of his trusted councilors to bring him before him.

He came and entered into the presence of Pharaoh, and did obeisance to him as it is fitting to do to kings, and he said to him, "My lord the king, Ashurbanipal the king hails you with abundance of peace and might, and honor. He has sent me, who is one of his servants, that I may answer you your questions, and may fulfill all your desire, for you have sent a message to my lord the king seeking a man who will build you a castle between the sky and the earth. I, through the help of the Highest God and your noble favor and the power of my lord the king will build it for you as you desire. But, my lord king, what you have said about the tribute of Egypt for three years, now the stability of a kingdom is strict justice, and if you win and my hand has no skill in replying to you,

107

then my lord the king will send you the tribute which you have mentioned. If I will have answered you in your questions, it will remain for you to send whatever you have mentioned to my lord the king."

When Pharaoh heard that speech, he wondered and was perplexed by the freedom of his tongue and the pleasantness of his speech. King Pharaoh asked him, "Man, what is your name?"

He answered, "Your servant is Abi Qam, and I am but a little ant among the ants of King Ashurbanipal."

Pharaoh said to him, "Has your lord no one of higher dignity than you, that he has sent me a little ant to reply to me, and to talk with me?"

Ahikar said to him, "My lord king! I will pray to God Highest that I may fulfill what is on your mind, for God is with the weak that he may confound the strong."

Then Pharaoh commanded that they should prepare a living place for Abi Qam and supply him with provisions, meat, and drink, and all that he needed. When it was finished, three days afterward Pharaoh clothed himself in purple and red and sat on his throne, and all his viziers and the magnates of his kingdom were standing with their hands crossed, their feet close together, and their heads bowed.

Pharaoh sent to fetch Abi Qam, and when he was presented to him, he did obeisance before him, and kissed the ground in front of him. King Pharaoh asked him, "Abi Qam, who am I like? And the nobles of my kingdom, who are they like?"

Ahikar answered him, "My lord king, you are like the god Bel, and the nobles of your kingdom are like his servants."

He said to him, "Go, and come back here tomorrow."

So Ahikar left as king Pharaoh had commanded him. In the morning, Ahikar returned into the presence of Pharaoh, and did obeisance, and stood before the king. Pharaoh was dressed in a red, and the nobles were dressed in white. Pharaoh asked him, "Abi Qam, who am I like? And the nobles of my kingdom, who are they like?"

Ahikar answered him, "My lord, you are like the sun, and your servants are like its beams."

Pharaoh replied to him, "Go to your home, and return here tomorrow."

Then Pharaoh commanded his court to wear pure white, and Pharaoh was dressed like them and sat on his throne, and he commanded them to fetch Ahikar. He entered and sat down before him, and Pharaoh asked him, "Abi Qam, who am I like? And my nobles, who are they like?"

Abi Qam answered him, "My lord, you are like the moon, and your nobles are like the planets and the stars."

Pharaoh replied to him, "Go, and tomorrow return here."

Then Pharaoh commanded his servants to wear robes of various colors, and Pharaoh wore a red velvet dress, and sat on his throne, and commanded them to bring in Abi Qam. He entered and did obeisance before him, and he asked, "Abi Qam, who am I like? And my armies, who are they like?"

He answered, "My lord, you are like the month of Parmoute,[1] and your armies are like its flowers."

When the king heard it he rejoiced greatly and said, "The first time you compared me to the idol Bel, and my nobles to his servants. The second time you compared me to the sun, and my nobles to the sunbeams. The third time you compared me to the moon, and my nobles to the planets and the stars. The fourth time you compared me to the month of Parmoute, and my nobles to its flowers. But now, Abi Qam, tell me, your lord King Ashurbanipal, who is he like? And his nobles, who are they like?"

Ahikar shouted with a loud voice and said, "It is far from me to make mention of my lord the king, while you are seated on your throne. Get up on your feet that I may tell you who my lord the king is like and who his nobles are like."

Pharaoh was confused by the freedom of his words and his boldness in answering. Pharaoh rose from his throne, and stood before Ahikar, and said, "Tell me now, that I may know who your lord the king is like, and who his nobles are like."

Ahikar said to him, "My lord is the sky god, and his nobles are the lightning and the thunder, and when he wills it, the winds blow and the rain falls. He commands the thunder, and there is lightning and rain, and he holds the Sun, and it does not give its light, and the moon and the stars, and they don't circle. He commands the tempest, and it blows and the rain falls and it tramples in Parmoute and destroys its flowers and its houses."

When Pharaoh heard this speech, he was very confused and was extremely angry, and said to him, "Man, tell me the truth, and let me know who you really are."

He admitted the truth, "I am Ahikar the scribe, greatest of the trusted councilors of King Ashurbanipal, and I am his vizier and the governor of his kingdom, and his chancellor."

He said to him, "You have told the truth in this saying. But we have heard that king Ashurbanipal has executed Ahikar, yet you seem to be alive and well."

Ahikar answered him, "Yes, so it was, but praise be to God, who knows what is hidden, for my lord the king commanded me to be killed, and he believed the lies told of men, but the Lord saved me, and blessed is he who trusts in him."

Pharaoh said to Ahikar, "Go, and tomorrow return here, and tell me something that I have never heard from my nobles or the people of my kingdom and my country."

RESTORATION: CHAPTER 5 NOTES

1 Greek: Farmouṭi (Φαρμουθί)
- Armenian: Pôarmutôi (Փարմուͳի)
- Arabic: Baramūdah (برموده)

111

Pȧ-ėn-rėnėn-wėtėt (𓊪𓈖𓂋𓈖𓏤𓅱𓏏𓏏) was the eighth month of the Egyptian civil calendar, and the last month of the Season of the Emergence (𓇷𓏏), when the Nile floods receded and the crops started to grow. It continued into the Coptic calendars as Parmoute (Παρμογτε) and Farmouṭi (Φαρμογθι). This month is approximately April 9 to May 8 on the Gregorian calendar during the 21st century. It is generally translated as Parmoute in English from the Sahidic dialect of Coptic.

RESTORATION: CHAPTER 6

Ahikar returned to his residence, and wrote a letter, saying in it on this:

"From King Ashurbanipal of Nineveh in Assyria to Pharaoh king of Egypt.

Peace be on you, my brother!

Let us make known to you through this message that a brother needs his brother, and kings of each other, and my hope from you is that you would lend me nine hundred talents of gold, for I need it for the provisioning of some of the soldiers, and I will spend it on them. At some point, I will return it to you."

Then he folded the letter and presented it in the morning to Pharaoh. When he saw it, he was confused and said to him, "I have never heard anything like these words from anyone."

Then Ahikar said to him, "Truly this is a debt which you owe to my lord the king."

Pharaoh accepted this, saying, "Ahikar, it is your way to be honest in the service of kings. Blessed be God who has made you perfect in wisdom and has adorned you with philosophy and knowledge. Now, Ahikar, there remains what we desire from you, that you should build as a castle between the sky and earth."

Then Ahikar replied, "To hear is to obey. I will build you a castle as you wish, but, my lord I will need lime, stone, clay, and workmen prepared. I have skilled builders who will build it for you as you desire."

The king prepared everything for him, and they went to a wide place where Ahikar also came, and he took the eagles and the young boys with him. The king and all his nobles went and the whole city assembled, that they might see what Ahikar would do. Then Ahikar let the eagles out of the boxes, and tied the young men on their backs, and tied the ropes to the eagles' feet, and let them go in the air. They soared upwards, till they were between the sky and earth.

The boys began to shout, saying, "Bring bricks, bring clay, that we may build the king's castle, for we are standing idle!"

The crowd was astonished and perplexed, and they wondered. The king and his nobles wondered. Ahikar and his servants began to beat the workmen, and they shouted for the king's troops, saying to them, "Bring the skilled workmen what they want and do not stop them from their work."

The king said to him, "You are mad, who can bring anything up to that height?"

Ahikar said to him, "My lord, how will we build a castle in the air? If my lord the king were here, he would have built several castles in a single day."

Pharaoh said to him, "Leave Ahikar, to your residence, and rest. We have given up building the castle, but tomorrow return to me."

Then Ahikar went to his residence and in the morning he returned to Pharaoh, and Pharaoh said, "Ahikar, what news is there of the horse of your lord? When he neighs in Nineveh in the country of Assyria, and our mares hear his voice, they abandon their young."

When Ahikar heard this riddle he went and took a cat, and tied her up and began to flog her violently until the Egyptians heard it, and they went and told the king about it. Pharaoh sent for Ahikar, and said to him, "Ahikar, why do you flog and beat that dumb animal?"

Ahikar said to him, my lord the king, she has done an ugly deed to me and has deserved this beating and flogging, for my lord King Ashurbanipal had given me a fine rooster, and he had a strong true voice and knew the hours of the day and the night. The cat got up this very night and bit off its head and went away, and because of this deed I have beaten her."

Pharaoh said to him, "Ahikar, I see from all this that you are growing old and are losing your mind, for between Egypt and Nineveh there are sixty-eight iterus,[1] and how did she go this very night and cut off the head of your rooster and returned?"

Ahikar said to him, "My lord, if there is such a distance between Egypt and Nineveh how could your mares hear when my lord the king's horse neighs and abandon their young? How could the voice of the horse reach Egypt?"

115

When Pharaoh heard that, he knew that Ahikar had answered his riddle, and Pharaoh said, "Ahikar, I want you to make me ropes from the sea-sand."

Ahikar said to him, "My lord king, order them to bring me a rope out of the treasury that I may make one like it."

Then Ahikar went to the back of the house, and drilled holes in the rough shape of the sea, and took a handful of sand in his hand, sea-sand. When the sun rose and shone through the holes, he spread the sand in the sun till it looked like woven like ropes. Ahikar said, "Command your servants to take these ropes, and whenever you desire it, I will weave you some more like them."

Pharaoh said, "Ahikar, we have a millstone here and it has been broken and I want you to sew it up."

Then Ahikar looked at it and found another stone. He said, "My lord, I am a foreigner, and I have no tool for sewing. But I want you to command your faithful shoemakers to cut awls from this stone, that I may sew that millstone."

Then Pharaoh and all his nobles laughed. He said, "Blessed be the Highest God, who gave you this wit and knowledge."

When Pharaoh saw that Ahikar had overcome him, and answered his riddles, he at once became excited and commanded them to collect for him three years' tribute and to bring them to Ahikar. He stripped off his robes and put them on Ahikar, and his soldiers, and his servants, and gave him the expenses of his journey. He said to him, "Go in peace, strength of your lord and pride of your teachers. Have any of the kingSultans your like? Give my greetings to your lord King Ashurbanipal, and say to him how we have sent him gifts, for kings are content with little."

Then Ahikar arose, and kissed king Pharaoh's hands and kissed the ground in front of him, and wished him strength and continuance, and abundance in his treasury, and said to him, "My lord, I desire from you that not one of our countrymen may remain in Egypt."

Pharaoh rose and sent heralds to proclaim in the streets of Egypt that not one of the people of Nineveh in Assyria should remain in the land of Egypt, but that they should go with Ahikar. Then Ahikar left King Pharaoh and traveled to Nineveh in the land of Assyria and he had some treasures and a great deal of wealth.

When the news reached King Ashurbanipal that Ahikar was coming, he went out to meet him and rejoiced over him exceedingly with great joy and embraced him and kissed him and said to him, "Welcome home, my relative, my brother Ahikar, the strength of my kingdom, and pride of my realm. Ask what you would have from me, even if you desire half of my kingdom and my possessions."

Then Ahikar said to him, "My lord king, live forever! Show favor, my lord king, to Abi Samik instead of me, for my life was in the hands of God and also his."

Then King Ashurbanipal said, "Honor be to you, my beloved Ahikar! I will make the station of Abi Samik the swordsman, higher than all my trusted councilors and my favorites."

Then the king began to ask him how he had dealt with Pharaoh from when he arrived until he had left his presence, and how he had answered all his questions, and how he had received the tribute from him, and the changes of clothing and the presents. King Ashurbanipal celebrated with great joy, and said to Ahikar, "Take what you would have of this tribute, for it is all within your hands."

Ahikar replied, "Let the king live forever! I desire nothing but the safety of my lord king and the continuance of his greatness. My lord, what can I do with wealth and its like? But if you will show me favor, give me Nadan, my sister's son, that I may repay him for what he has done to me, and grant me his blood and hold me guiltless of it."

Ashurbanipal the king said, "Take him, I have given him to you."

Ahikar took Nadan, his sister's son, and bound his hands with chains of iron, and took him to his home, and put heavy shackles on his feet, and tied it with a tight knot, and after binding him so he threw him into a dark room, beside the retiring-place, and appointed Nebu-hal as watchman over him to give him a loaf of bread and a little water every day.

RESTORATION: CHAPTER 6 NOTES

1 Aramaic: prśhå (ﬡﬣﬡﬢ). Translation: parasang (or league)

• Greek: parasángēs (παρασάγγης). Translation: parasang (or league)

• Armenian: hrasax (Հրասախ). Translation: parasang (or league)

• Arabic: farsaḵ (فَرْسَخ). Translation: parasang (or league)

The unit of measurement used in the text was the parasang, a Persian unit that was adopted by many other cultures. The term is accepted as having been adopted by other cultures during the Persian era, meaning it must have been a Persian era replacement for an older term. Its length was not consistent, ranging between 4.8 and 5.6 km (3 to 3½ miles). The term could not have been the original term in the text, as 68 parasangs would have only been about 340 km (200 miles), while the distance from the Egyptian capital of Sais to Nineveh would have been 1500 to 1600 kilometers (900 to 1000 miles), depending on the route taken.

The earlier Mesopotamian unit of measurement which is also translated into English as 'league,' was the bêr (𒁉𒌑), which was approximately 2.7 km (1.7 miles) long, even shorter than the parasang. The text implies that the original unit of measurement that the king of Egypt used, was very long as there were only 68 of them between Egypt and Assyria. The longest Egyptian unit of measurement that appears to have been used at the time was the îtrw (𓇋𓏤𓈗𓏤), which is translated into English as the "River-Measure League," as it was a nautical distance. It was approximately 10.5 km (6.5 miles) long, which would make the distance listed approximately 714 km (444 miles), which is only half the distance from Sais to Nineveh. As the unit of measurement was nautical, and the distance mentioned was approximately the distance from Sais to the Assyrian ports in Lebanon, it is plausible that the original text was referring to the Assyrian Empire, and not the city of Nineveh itself.

RESTORATION: CHAPTER 7

Whenever Ahikar went in or out, he chastised Nadan, his sister's son, saying, "Nadan, my boy, I have done to you all that is good and kind and you have rewarded me for it, with what is ugly and bad and with murder. My son, it is said in the proverbs, 'He who does not listen with his ears, they will make listen with the scruff of his neck.'"

Nadan asked, "Why are you angry with me?"

Ahikar said to him, "Because I raised you, and taught you, and gave you honor and respect and made you great, and reared you with the best of breeding, and seated you in my place that you might be my heir in the world, and you treated me with killing and repaid me with my ruin. But the Lord knew that I was wronged, and he saved me from the trap which you had set for me, for the Lord heals the broken hearts and hinders the envious and the haughty.

My boy, you have been to me like the scorpion which when it strikes on brass, pierces it.

My boy, you are like the gazelle who was eating the roots of the madder, and it adds to me today, but tomorrow they will tan they hide in my roots.

My boy, you have been like he who saw his comrade naked in the winter, and he took cold water and poured it on him.

My boy, you have been to me like a man who took a stone and threw it up to the sky to stone the Lord with it. The stone did not hit and did not reach high enough, but it became the cause of guilt and sin.

My boy, if you had honored me and respected me and had listened to my words you would have been my heir and would have reigned over my dominions.

My son, know that if the tail of the dog or the pig were ten cubits long it would not approach the worth of the horse's even if it were like silk.

My boy! I thought that you would have been my heir at my death, and you through your envy and your insolence desired to kill me. But the Lord delivered me from your cunning.

My son, you have been to me like a trap which was set up on the dunghill, and there came a sparrow and found the trap set up. The sparrow asked the trap, "Why are you here?"

The trap answered, "I am praying here to God."

The lark also asked it, "What is the piece of wood that you hold?"

The trap replied, "That is a young oak-tree on which I lean at the time of prayer."

The lark asked, "What is that thing in your mouth?"

The trap answered, "That is bread and meat which I carry for all the hungry and the poor who come near to me."

The lark asked, "Now then, may I come forward and eat, as I am hungry?"

The trap answered him, "Come forward."

The lark approached so it might eat, but the trap sprang up and seized the lark by its neck. The lark answered and said to the trap, "If that is your bread for the hungry God will not accept your alms and your kind deeds. If that is your fasting and your prayers, God accepts from you neither your fast or your prayer, and God will not perfect what is good concerning you."

My boy, you have been to me like a lion who made friends with a donkey, and the donkey kept walking before the lion for a time, and one day the lion sprang on the donkey and ate it up.

My boy, you have been to me like a weevil in the wheat, for it does nothing good, but spoils the wheat and eats it.

My boy, you have been like a man who sowed ten measures of wheat, and when it was harvest time, he arose and reaped it, and separated it, and threshed it, and struggled over it to the utmost, and it turned out to be ten measures, and its master said to it, "You lazy thing, you have not grown and you have not shrunk."

My boy, you have been to me like the partridge that had been thrown into the net, and she could not save herself, but she called out to the partridges, that she might get them caught in the net with her.

My son, you have been to me like the cold dog and it went into the potter's house to get warm. When it had gotten warm, it began to bark at them, and they chased it out and beat it, that it might not bite them.

My son, you have been to me like the pig who went into the hot bath with people of quality, and when it came out of the hot bath, it saw a muddy hole and it went down and wallowed in it.

My son, you have been to me like the goat which joined its comrades on their way to the sacrifice, and it was unable to save itself.

My boy, the dog which is not fed through its hunting becomes food for flies.

My son, the hand which does not labor and plow and is greedy and cunning will be cut away from its shoulder.

My son, the eye in which light is not seen, the ravens will pick at it and pluck it out.

My boy, you have been to me like a tree whose branches they were cutting, and it said to them, "If something of me were not in your hands, verily you would be unable to cut me."

My boy, you are like the cat to who they said, "Stop stealing until we make you a chain of gold and feed you with sugar and almonds."

She replied, "I am not forgetful of the craft of my father and my mother."

My son, you have been like the serpent riding on a thorn-bush when he was among a river, and a wolf saw them and said, "Mischief on mischief, and let him who is more mischievous than they direct both of them."

The serpent said to the wolf, "The lambs and the goats and the sheep which you have eaten all your life, will you return them to their fathers and their parents or not?"

The wolf answered, "No."

The serpent said to him, "I think that after myself you are the worst of us."

My boy, I fed you with good food and you did not feed me with dry bread.

My boy, I gave you sugared water to drink and good syrup, and you did not give me water from the well to drink.

My boy, I taught you and raised you, and you dug a hiding-place for me and hid me.

My boy, I brought you up with the best upbringing and trained you like a tall cedar, and you have twisted and bent me.

My boy, it was my hope concerning you that you would build me a fortified castle, that I might be concealed from my enemies in it, and you did become to me like one buried in the depth of the earth, but the Lord took pity on me and delivered me from your cunning.

My boy, I wished you well, and you did reward me with evil and hatefulness, and now I would fain tear from your eyes, and make you food for dogs, and cut out your tongue, and take off your head with the edge of the sword, and repay you for your abominable deeds."

When Nadan heard this speech from his uncle Ahikar, he said, "My uncle! Deal with me according to your knowledge, and forgive my sins, for who is there who has sinned like me, or who is there who forgives like you? Accept me, my uncle! Now I will serve in your house, and groom your horses and sweep up the dung of your livestock, and feed your sheep, for I am wicked and you are righteous. I the guilty and you the forgiving."

Ahikar answered him, "My boy, you are like the tree which was fruitless beside the water, and its master decided to cut it down, and it said to him, 'Move me to another place, and if I do not carry fruit, cut me down.'

Its master said to it, 'You've been beside the water and have not borne fruit, how will you carry fruit when you are in another place?'

My boy, the old age of the eagle is better than the youth of the crow.

My boy, they told the wolf, 'Keep away from the sheep in case their dust should harm you.' The wolf said, 'The dregs of the sheep's milk are good for my eyes.'

My boy, they made the wolf go to a school so he might learn to read and they said to him, 'Say A, B...' He said, 'Lamb, goat...'

My boy, they set the donkey down at the table and he fell and began to roll himself in the dust and one said, "Let him roll himself, for it is his nature, he will not change."

My boy, the saying has been confirmed which goes, 'If you beget a boy, call him your son, and if you teach a boy, call him your slave.'

My boy, he who does good, will meet with good; and he who does evil will meet with evil, for the Lord repays a man according to the measure of his work.

My boy, what will I say more to you than these sayings? The Lord knows what is hidden, and is acquainted with the mysteries and the secrets. He will repay you and will judge, between me and you, and will repay you according to all your deserve."

When Nadan heard that speech from his uncle Ahikar, he swelled up immediately and became like a blown-out canteen. His limbs swelled and his legs and his feet and his side, and he was torn and his belly burst and his intestines were scattered, and he died. His end was destruction, and he went to the grave. For he who digs a pit for his brother will fall into it, and he who sets up traps will be caught in them.

This is what happened and what we found about the Words of Ahikar. Praise God forever. Amen, and peace.

This chronicle is finished with the help of God, may he be praised!

Amen, Amen, Amen.

ALSO AVAILABLE

ALSO AVAILABLE

- Septuagint: History, Volume 2

- Octateuch: The Original Orit

ENOCH AND METATRON SERIES:
- Books of Enoch Collection

- Books of Enoch and Metatron Collection

- Books of Metatron Collection

- Secrets of Enoch

OTHER TRANSLATIONS:
- Apocalypses of Ezra

- Arabic Maccabees

- Hebrew Maccabees

- Life of Adam and Eve

- Memories of the New Kingdom

- Septuagint's Esther and the Vetus Latina Esther

- Septuagint's Ezekiel and the Ba'al Cycle

- Septuagint's Job and the Testament of Job

- Septuagint's Proverbs and the Wisdom of Amenemope

- The Amarna Letters

- Testaments of the Patriarchs Collection

- Tobit and Ahikar

- Ugaritic Texts: Ba'al Cycle

- Wisdom of Ahikar

www.ingramcontent.com/pod-product-compliance
Lightning Source LLC
Chambersburg PA
CBHW071158120626
46546CB00006B/2327